Learning
— by —
Mistake

ASCD MEMBER BOOK

Many ASCD members received this book
as a member benefit upon its initial release.

Learn more at **www.ascd.org/memberbooks**

Learning
— by —
Mistake

12 Strategies
to Turn Student Errors
into Opportunities

EMMA CHIAPPETTA

ascd
Arlington, Virginia USA

2111 Wilson Boulevard, Suite 300 • Arlington, VA 22201 USA
Phone: 800-933-2723 or 703-578-9600
Website: www.ascd.org • Email: member@ascd.org
Author guidelines: www.ascd.org/write

Richard Culatta, *Chief Executive Director;* Anthony Rebora, *Chief Content Officer;* Genny Ostertag, *Managing Director, Book Acquisitions and Editing;* Susan Hills, *Senior Acquisitions Editor;* Mary Beth Nielsen, *Director, Book Editing;* Jamie Greene, *Senior Editor;* Masie Chong, *Senior Graphic Designer;* Circle Graphics, *Typesetter;* Kelly Marshall, *Production Manager;* Shajuan Martin, *E-Publishing Specialist*

PAPERBACK ISBN: 978-1-4166-3382-2   ASCD product #125011
PDF EBOOK ISBN: 978-1-4166-3383-9; see Books in Print for other formats.
Quantity discounts are available: email programteam@ascd.org or call 800-933-2723, ext. 5773, or 703-575-5773. For desk copies, go to www.ascd.org/deskcopy.

ASCD Member Book No. FY25-5 (July 2025 PSI+). ASCD Member Books mail to Premium (P), Select (S), and Institutional Plus (I+) members on this schedule: Jan, PSI+; Feb, P; Apr, PSI+; May, P; Jul, PSI+; Aug, P; Sep, PSI+; Nov, PSI+; Dec, P. For current details on membership, see www.ascd.org/membership.

Library of Congress Cataloging-in-Publication Data
Names: Chiappetta, Emma author
Title: Learning by mistake : 12 strategies to turn student errors into opportunities / Emma Chiappetta.
Other titles: 12 strategies to turn student errors into opportunities
Description: Arlington, Virginia : ASCD, [2025]
Identifiers: LCCN 2025011978 (print) | LCCN 2025011979 (ebook) | ISBN 9781416633822 paperback | ISBN 9781416633839 pdf
Subjects: LCSH: Teaching | Errors
Classification: LCC LB1025.3 .C4537 2025 (print) | LCC LB1025.3 (ebook) | DDC 371.102/3—dc23/eng/20250616
LC record available at https://lccn.loc.gov/2025011978
LC ebook record available at https://lccn.loc.gov/2025011979

31 30 29 28 27 26 25   1 2 3 4 5 6 7 8 9 10 11 12

Learning
— by —
Mistake

Creating a Positive Mistake Culture

Sarah, a senior in my calculus class at the time, shared her anxiety about mistakes with me near the start of the school year.

"Making mistakes can be super-stressful," she said. "I feel as though I will be called out in front of everyone even though the likelihood of that is very, very small." I could even hear the thirst for perfection in her tone.

Sarah was one of the highest-performing students in the school, so naturally I wondered if her anxiety was unique to her or if it was pervasive among her peers. I began to informally interview my students about their attitudes surrounding mistakes and planned to revisit these conversations at the end of the school year to measure growth. I made a point to ask students, "What is it like to make a mistake at school?" One after another, they described how "scary" or "embarrassing" it feels to "mess up in front of everyone." At the same time, they noted that they thought it was possible to learn from mistakes, recalling times when making an error just once led them to never make it again.

There is a disconnect here. How can students be so terrified of making mistakes while also appreciating how valuable mistakes can be to learning? How much learning are they missing out on because of this fear? This book explores these questions and provides actionable strategies that every teacher can use to change the culture around mistakes in the classroom. Each chapter of the book focuses on one strategy, activity, or lesson that teachers can implement to ensure their students see making mistakes as commonplace, expected, and merit-worthy. Examples are drawn from all grade levels and subject areas.

How Mistakes Cause Anxiety

Grace started to become aware of her identity and the impact she had on others around 2nd grade. Her parents emphasized the importance of school, and she had learned to value the idea of being "smart."

One day in class, as she and her classmates were taking turns reading aloud, Grace stumbled on a word. She struggled to sound it out and ultimately it came out all wrong.

"Grace, how could you miss that word?" her teacher exclaimed. "It was on our spelling quiz last week!"

Her classmates giggled. Grace's cheeks flushed, and her ears got hot. She heard a buzzing sound in her head and couldn't focus for the rest of the class.

The next time Grace needed to participate in a read-aloud, she immediately got all the same physical symptoms of anxiety. She looked ahead in the passage to predict which section she would need to read and made sure she knew every word beforehand. She didn't even listen to her classmates because she was practicing her paragraph over and over in her head.

In 3rd grade, Grace's mistake anxiety grew. Whenever the class practiced multiplication tables out loud, for example, she was afraid of getting hers wrong. Would her teacher be disappointed? Would her classmates laugh again? These worries caused her to practice her multiplication at home every night. However, she rarely volunteered answers in class, and she would never even try to answer one of the harder word problems at the board. When she got some of the more challenging problems wrong on a test, she was punished with a bad grade and needed to bring the test home for her parents to sign.

By the time Grace got to high school, she had high expectations for herself and an intense need to present herself as the perfect student, which only added to her anxiety. Once, when she was working on an essay for AP Literature, she was so worried about her grade that she had an AI program generate the essay and submitted it verbatim.

Typically, students begin to develop anxiety about making mistakes early on in school (Harouni, 2022). The response they receive after making their first few errors can affect how they view mistake-making forever. If that response is negative, as in Grace's case, students may become anxious anytime they face the prospect of making a mistake. And if responses to their mistakes continue to be negative, that anxiety can increase over time. Eventually, students may stop even trying and give in to plagiarism or use AI to complete assignments.

The Four Main Levers of Mistake Response

Although a deep fear of being wrong can be crippling, it is certainly not insurmountable—and since we as teachers control the consequences of student mistakes, we can help ensure that they don't cause anxiety in the first place. Of course, chances are that you won't be present when a student makes their first mistake, but you can still do a lot to lessen their anxiety. The most effective treatment is safe exposure: making mistakes in a safe environment and observing that fears of negative consequences were either baseless or vastly overblown. Providing students with safe exposure to mistakes is key to building a healthy culture around mistakes in our classrooms.

As soon as a student makes a mistake, there are four main levers of response that help decide whether the student will catalog the event as traumatic or as a learning experience (see Figure 1.1).

Consequences

There are many different forms of consequences that can result from our actions. One such form is punishment, whose purpose is to condemn

Figure 1.1

The Four Levers of Mistake Response

Lever	Traumatic	Learning Experience
Consequences	• Lower grade • Loss of privileges • Verbal reprimand • Punishment	• Revision opportunities • No grade penalty on formative assessments
Teacher Reactions	• Disappointment • Anger • Dismissiveness	• Enthusiasm • Curiosity • Validation
Teacher Strategies	• Emphasize perfection	• Create safe mistake-making experiences
Peer Reactions	• Laughter • Taunting • Isolation	• Enthusiasm • Curiosity • Validation

a behavior and discourage it from happening again. Naturally, punishing mistakes results in a feeling of condemnation and an aversion to making them. Students learn that it's better not to try at all than to be wrong.

Punishment comes in many shapes, including reprimands ("How could you have forgotten this? I went over it 10 times!") and the removal of privileges. However, the most common form of punishment comes in the form of grades.

One student I interviewed told me she feels the most anxious in her core courses because they're the ones "that seriously matter for college." She isn't as concerned about making mistakes in pass/fail elective courses since she knows she can still pass without being perfect. Students fear mistakes most when the stakes are highest.

The same student told me that her anxiety prevented her from stretching out and taking chances in core classes. She always wrote "the essay that her teacher would like" rather than the one she really wanted to write, or she took on a project she thought would be easier to ace than one that might be more interesting but likely more of a challenge.

When students are given some space to make mistakes without it affecting their grade, they feel more comfortable taking risks and challenging themselves. This doesn't mean that students should make tons of mistakes on summative assessments, but they need plenty of formative opportunities to be creative, try new things, experiment, and practice without fear of it affecting their transcript.

Teacher Reactions

Students look to teachers for validation and as models of appropriate behavior and attitudes. If a student makes a mistake and the teacher seems disappointed, upset, or angry, the student (and their classmates) will believe that these are the appropriate responses and that mistakes are to be avoided at all costs. If, on the other hand, the teacher seems interested, intrigued, or excited about the learning opportunity presented by the mistake, the student who made it will feel validated, and their classmates will be less afraid to make mistakes as well.

Even a simple response like "That's not it. Can someone help him out?" can be discouraging. Instead, saying something like "That's an interesting thought. How did you come up with it?" can show students that even though they were wrong, their thoughts are still valuable and productive.

Teacher Strategies

In addition to reacting enthusiastically the moment a mistake is made, teachers can do a lot to prepare for and follow up on student mistakes. Much of this book is dedicated to strategies and activities that teachers can use to proactively create a positive culture around mistakes. In addition to a detailed description of an intentional mistake-making exercise, each chapter includes FAQs and a selection of related resources.

Peer Reactions

Young people are especially attuned to how their peers perceive them. Being accepted, making friends, and asserting identity hugely influence student behavior. If classmates burst into laughter, say mean things, or even silently snicker when a student makes a mistake, that student will surely view the event as traumatic. Effects might be felt outside the class-room, too. For example, if students begin to think of a classmate who makes mistakes as "dumb," they might tease that student on the play-ground or avoid sitting with them at the lunch table.

Although peer reactions are difficult for teachers to control, shaping the classroom's overall attitude to mistakes can have a major impact. If a teacher sets a strong example and creates a culture where mistakes are valued and viewed as critical to learning, students will be less likely to taunt or isolate mistake-making classmates.

By creating classroom experiences that turn each lever of mistake response in the direction of a positive culture, we can completely change our students' perceptions of making mistakes. I've seen it myself. By the end of the school year, the students I had interviewed developed a dif-ferent attitude about being wrong, at least in the classroom community we had co-created. One said, "In this class, I'm more likely to realize my mistakes and correct them." Another said, "I talk and answer questions more in your class because I feel like it's safe here."

Anxiety around mistakes is pervasive, and we all have to make an effort to change the culture around mistake making if we want to have a lasting effect on our students. The strategies in this book represent just a few ways to move the four levers in the right direction. However, before implementing these strategies, you must understand and truly believe in the value of making mistakes.

The Value of Making Mistakes

Before moving on, I want to be clear: the desire to avoid making mistakes is *not* a bad thing. It can cause students to study harder, check their work, and be more careful, as it did for Grace. And there are many scenarios outside school in which making a mistake really could be terrible. For example, if a surgeon is operating on you, you don't want them thinking, "If I mess this up, it'll be a great learning opportunity!" However, you *would* want your surgeon to be able to practice surgery in a setting where mistakes are OK.

We want our students to be able to write great essays and solve difficult problems without making mistakes. We want them to be successful on high-stakes exams, perform well in the school play, and flawlessly execute a musical piece. Ideally, students perform at a high level with as few mistakes as possible in the moments when doing so really counts—but they need a safe space to play, mess up, experiment, and be creative along the way. Mistakes have the most value during the learning process, which is messy, circuitous, and unpredictable.

What the Research Says

There is so much literature out there on this topic that I hardly believe I can do justice to it here. However, it's important to note that making mistakes literally primes us for deeper learning.

In a 2018 magnetic resonance imaging (MRI) study, neuroscientists at the California Institute of Technology examined the effects of making a mistake on brain activity. Within 50 milliseconds of a participant making a mistake, they observed a group of "conflict neurons" fire in quick succession. This is the exact type of activity that allows our brains to encode information more deeply (Terada, 2020). We can't all see inside our neural pathways, but we have likely felt this sensation before. Making a mistake reveals a gap in our knowledge and signals us to actively seek the information that will fill the gap.

One of my favorite research studies, by Cyr and Anderson (2018), asked participants to recall Spanish words and their English equivalents. Some of the pairs were cognates, such as *accidente/accident*. Others were false cognates, such as *ropa/clothes*. Half the participants learned the pairs through rote memorization, whereas the other half just guessed the English equivalent of the Spanish word. The study showed that subjects in the latter group showed greater retention of the paired words, especially when their initial guess was wrong!

Cyr and Anderson's study reveals the power of being wrong. It can cause a light in your brain to turn on, signaling that you need to learn something. Imagine the power of this in the classroom. Taking a pretest, even one where students answer every question incorrectly, causes students to become curious about filling the gaps in their knowledge that the pretest exposes.

Mistakes do not always lead to learning—for example, if the person making the mistake doesn't realize they've made one, they will likely continue to make the same mistake. Repetition of any action or thought causes the neural pathways for that action or thought to become stronger. If a student repeatedly makes the same mistake, the brain builds a strong neural pathway toward a wrong answer. Similarly, if a teacher simply corrects a student without providing any learning support, the student might be less likely to risk making a wrong answer next time, or a student might make a mistake but fail to put in the work to learn the correct answer.

For students to learn from mistakes, there needs to be an acknowledgment of the mistake, intentional learning around correcting it, and reflection about where the mistake came from, why it is wrong, and how it can be avoided in the future (Cohen, 2020). Students in classrooms where mistakes are welcomed, analyzed, learned from, and reflected on have better academic outcomes than those in environments where mistakes are frowned upon and punished (Steuer et al., 2013).

A healthy approach to mistake-making can have effects that reach far beyond the classroom. Creative ideas blossom when freedom of thought is welcomed. I once had the chance to participate in a brainstorm following the "Yes, and" protocol: after one person shared an idea, the next person would respond, "Yes, and," and add onto the idea. Though some of the ideas were outlandish, the knowledge that we wouldn't be shut down and that colleagues would build on our ideas was incredibly freeing.

This freedom is what students feel in a classroom with a positive mistake culture. In addition to making learning gains, they aren't afraid to be wrong or take risks, are willing to collaborate and offer brilliantly creative ideas, and solve problems more effectively.

In the next 12 chapters, we'll explore a dozen strategies and classroom activities that will help you build a healthy mistake culture and bolster learning by analyzing and reflecting on mistakes. Let's dive in.

2

Addressing the Fear of Making Mistakes

Take a moment to reflect on the tone you want to set around mistakes in your classroom. How do you want your students to respond to their own mistakes? To their classmates' mistakes? How do *you* want to respond to students' mistakes? How do you want students to feel while and after making a mistake? The beginning of the school year is an ideal time to set the tone you desire. In this chapter, we'll discuss how to do just that.

In a classroom with a healthy mistake culture, students take risks without fear of being wrong. Mistakes are treated as part of the learning process rather than as roadblocks or indicators of low intelligence. When students make mistakes, they don't feel embarrassed, shameful, or dejected. Instead, they are determined to figure out the truth and confident in their ability to do so. They know that if they can't get there on their own, their classmates and teacher will be there to support them.

Regardless of the grade level you teach, your students enter your class with a backpack full of previous mistake experiences. An important step in creating a healthy culture around mistake-making is understanding that baggage. In addition to giving a diagnostic test at the start of the year to discern your students' prior knowledge, I suggest using the strategies in this chapter to help determine the levels of mistake anxiety that your students carry.

"Wrong Answers Only"

Giving students the opportunity right off the bat to be wrong without suffering consequences will help you set a "Yes, and" tone. Such a tone will encourage students' creativity and desire to overcome their fear of mistakes. Ease them into this opportunity. Because students tend to carry mistake anxiety and perceive being wrong as shameful, you want to avoid putting them in a situation where they feel they are being forced into this uncomfortable state.

Consider the following example. You introduce a pop quiz on the previous year's content with something like "Don't worry—mistakes are welcome here! I don't expect your answers to be correct, and this quiz is not graded." Then you ask a question and randomly call on each student to answer. Do you think your brief words will be enough to reduce their mistake anxiety? Doubtful. Students will probably feel pressured to perform or get overwhelmed and respond, "I don't know." Your comments may ease their fears about grades, but they will still feel anxious about how their peers perceive them, especially if this is a new class with new classmates. Building culture takes time, and a few words at the start of the year will not be enough to undo years of shame that have built up around mistakes.

Instead, implement the "Wrong Answers Only" activity to get your students making mistakes in the first week without fear. In this low-stakes game, based on a popular internet meme, students share silly, purposely wrong answers to a prompt—for example, "List three things you keep in your refrigerator." Brainstorming wrong answers lays the groundwork for building comfort with mistakes. Afterward, students can have conversations about why each silly answer was wrong. These discussions get students into the habit of analyzing mistakes and reflecting on where misconceptions come from.

This game addresses the four levers of mistake response (see the Introduction) in the following ways:

1. The activity refrains from punishing mistakes. In fact, it does quite the opposite by encouraging students to make mistakes on purpose. The activity plays the role of an ungraded icebreaker that is purely for fun.

2. The teacher's response to wrong answers throughout this game should be curiosity. They should encourage silly and creative responses and ask students how they came up with their ideas. Doing so demonstrates that the teacher is more interested in students' thought processes than in their final answer.

3. The game promotes the development of a safe environment for making mistakes.

4. Students are encouraged to express curiosity about their peers' responses. The teacher should set a firm expectation that no response is to be ridiculed. Instead, the intention is to learn about how each group member came up with their idea.

If you are introducing this activity as an icebreaker early in the year, make sure that the prompts are not related to academic content to prevent students from feeling like they are being tested in front of their peers. Their fears about appearing "dumb" will arise even if there is no grade attached to the activity. I like to use silly prompts like these:

- Things you might find in a freezer
- Birthday party themes
- Vacation locations
- First date activities
- Sandwich ingredients
- The monster under the bed

In terms of format, you've got a few different options here. I prefer the energy and camaraderie that occur as students share their answers out loud, so I randomly assign students to small groups. Since students may not be comfortable having their name attached to their mistakes this early in the year, you may prefer answers to remain anonymous. This can be accomplished with a tool such as Poll Everywhere, which lets students submit responses via computer or text message and generates a word cloud. Then you can analyze the "wrongness" of each answer as a class and vote on which is "most wrong."

Before engaging in this activity, dedicate time for a conversation with your class about group work, norms, class routines, and respect. This lays the groundwork for a fun and harmless day in class. Then follow these steps:

1. Assign each small group to a whiteboard.

2. Present the prompt.

3. Give students three minutes to come up with as many wrong answers as they can. Have a scribe for the group write the answers on the whiteboard. (During each round of the game, a different student in each group plays the role of scribe.)

4. When the three minutes are up, each group spends an additional three minutes discussing all the answers and coming up with their favorite.

5. Each group shares its favorite answer with the whole class.

6. Repeat the process with a new prompt.

Following the game, have students individually fill out an anonymous survey about their attitudes toward making mistakes both in and out of school (see Figure 2.1). Data from the survey provide the teacher with diagnostic information about students' existing perceptions of mistakes as a starting point for the year.

Example

"Sneakers!"

"A cat wearing a scarf!"

"A severed finger!"

These are all responses I received to the prompt "Things you might find in a freezer." Of course, students had been asked to provide wrong answers only.

Figure 2.1

Sample Mistake Attitudes Survey

1. What is a mistake you made recently, either in or out of school?

2. How did it feel to make that mistake?

3. Did you learn anything from it?

4. How do you typically feel when you make a mistake in school?

5. How do you typically feel when you make a mistake outside school?

6. How do you react when you make a mistake?

7. Do you believe it's possible to learn from mistakes?

The room filled with giggles, and the responses became sillier and sillier. Students tossed them out at a rapid-fire pace, building on one another's energy. Kids who were normally quiet began to chime in, often more than once. By the time the game ended, students were nearly out of breath from laughing. I was excited for the year and hoped that we could build off this energy and comfort with one another to be creative, take risks, and confidently share "wrong" responses.

FAQs

Q: How can I prevent students from providing inappropriate responses?

A: When I first introduced this activity in class, I was terrified that my students might respond in ways that were inappropriate for school or culturally insensitive. The game is silly and encourages students to be funny or outlandish. Unfortunately, attempts at humor can too often lean on offensive stereotypes.

To help ensure that students steer clear of inappropriate language, facilitate a discussion about appropriate language and respectful communication the day before playing the game. Set clear expectations: "Your answers should be fun and creative, but make sure they are school appropriate." Then ask students what they think you mean by "school appropriate." After collectively defining that term with the class, provide an example prompt and ask students to silently think about what might make a response offensive. Ask them, "What are some qualities of responses that might hurt someone's feelings?" This can lead to a conversation about harmful stereotypes, what it means to respect one another, class norms, respect, and group work. You can also discuss fair consequences for breaking the norms.

When getting ready to play the game, have students repeat the expectations of respectful communication discussed the day before. While playing the game, if you hear any inappropriate responses, be sure to enforce the consequences that the class had previously decided upon.

Q: What can I do about students either dominating or not engaging in the activity?

A: If you find that some students are not participating in group discussions, remind the class about the previous day's discussion of norms for group work. Ask students how they would handle a situation in which some students don't contribute. They often have great ideas!

You can also join one of the groups and model the leadership qualities that you hope to see in your students. Seek out the quiet students and invite them to respond. After one of the engaged students responds, say something like "Great one! Now I'd love to hear what Ashe has to say!" You can also provide students with a minute of individual think time before the group sharing of ideas.

Another strategy is to empower group scribes to serve as conversation facilitators and ensure that everyone has an opportunity to share their responses. If the scribe rotates to a new member each round, everyone has a chance to facilitate and lead.

Q: How can I prevent students from different cultures from feeling left out?

A: Students from diverse cultural backgrounds might not feel included if they don't understand their classmates' cultural references. To mitigate this, try to come up with prompts that don't easily lend themselves to culture-specific responses (e.g., "sandwich ingredients," "places to hide your allowance") and avoid prompts that do (e.g., "celebrity babysitters").

Alternatively, you can encourage students to draw from their own cultures when responding to prompts. This gives them an opportunity to share a bit about their backgrounds and learn more about their classmates.

Conclusion

This chapter highlights the importance of setting a positive tone around mistakes early in the school year and offers a playful approach for doing so. The "Wrong Answers Only" lets students engage in low-stakes mistake-making that can help them shed the anxiety they associate with being wrong. By promoting curiosity, respect, and humor, this activity encourages them to see mistakes as nonthreatening and to feel comfortable contributing to the classroom community.

In the next chapter, we'll discuss a strategy that you use in the classroom every day—feedback—and how the language we use to provide it can affect mistake culture.

Additional Resources

- In this PBS video, White House speechwriter David Litt explains how finding humor in mistakes can help us move past them: www.youtube .com/watch?v=5WJhEoHWKo4
- This article from *The Atlantic* by Kieran Setiya can be used to initiate a discussion about how laughing with your friends about mistakes is a good way to destigmatize them: www.theatlantic.com/books /archive/2024/05/david-shoemaker-wisecracks/678471

3

The Effects of Teacher Feedback on Mistake-Making

Take a moment to reflect on some critical feedback that you have received. Who did it come from? What impact did it have on you? Why did it have that impact?

One of my favorite mathematics professors taught his class in the same style Peter Liljedahl recommends in his book *Building Thinking Classrooms* (2021). Students worked in groups as the professor walked around the room asking questions, scaffolding learning, and delivering feedback. His verbal feedback was always encouraging. His bubbly and energetic voice highlighted what was right about our thinking, and his questions let us know where we still needed to iron out some details. He never told us we were wrong; instead, he would encourage us to think of a counterexample to some claim we had made or to include more justification when we hadn't quite hit the mark yet. On written assignments, he typically scribbled more in the margins than each of us had written on the entire problem set. His comments were pointed, specific, and instructive but never punitive. In office hours, he would talk with me about my process and praise me for "thinking like a mathematician."

In this professor's class, I felt confident trying new things, even if I knew I'd make mistakes. My classmates and I learned to prod our own claims, consider counterexamples, and test our justifications out on one another. We took risks and were creative. We made mistakes and learned to catch them ourselves. The confidence he instilled in me encouraged me to become a math major, perform summer research, and even attend graduate school for math.

In graduate school, things were starkly different. I was rarely encouraged to speak in class. Questions were sparse, and we all felt embarrassed when we couldn't keep up with the professor's logic at the board. Feedback on problem sets mostly consisted of circles and Xs with a grade at the top of the paper. At first, I worked on problem sets with my peers, but when they started comparing grades, I didn't want to expose myself as possibly not doing as well as them. I was afraid to attend office hours for help, and when I finally mustered up the courage to go, rather than offering encouragement and support, my professor would scoff at my difficulty learning a particular theorem or piecing together the logic he had so clearly presented in class. He would take deep, exasperated breaths. I consistently felt his frustration, which quickly became my own.

I was so discouraged that, even though I had been planning on pursuing research in the field this professor taught, I balked and chose a different area. I didn't feel safe being wrong, so how could I do mathematical research, where the right answers aren't yet known, in such a context?

How we address our students' errors and misunderstandings matters deeply. There are whole libraries of books written about giving feedback, but in this chapter, we'll focus specifically on how to use feedback to foster a healthy culture around mistakes.

Using Feedback to Shape Students' Understanding

If you were a "good" student, you probably regularly received papers covered in checkmarks for each correct answer. You may have even gotten work back with a simple $A+$ or $\checkmark++$ at the top of your paper without a single splotch of red ink anywhere near your answers. However, when teachers hand back "perfect work" with nothing more than a slew of checkmarks, we miss a crucial opportunity to help students develop a growth mindset. At the same time, students who receive work back that is covered in red pen, circles, *X*s, and other marks feel like failures and subsequently shut down.

Feedback plays a critical role in shaping students' understanding of what teachers value in their work and guiding their growth in specific areas. In math, the subject I teach, we particularly value clarity, logical reasoning, creative problem-solving, perseverance, and curiosity. Thoughtfully crafted positive feedback can reinforce these key skills and qualities while also helping students understand which aspects of their approach are or aren't effective.

Demonstrating What We Value

Teachers often ask students to show their work so they can see their thought processes in action. It is valuable for us to understand how students are approaching the material. We can use feedback, especially positive feedback, to reinforce this behavior. For example:

- Your explanation here helps me see how you got from one step to the next.
- The picture you drew helps me understand how you're thinking about this.
- When you defined the variable before using it, I was able to follow your reasoning.
- The sentence at the end helps me see that this is your final answer.

Comments such as these acknowledge the effort students put into making their reasoning visible and validate their hard work.

Honoring Creativity

Across subject areas, it's critical for students to realize that there are often multiple "correct" ways to solve any problem. Feedback can highlight and celebrate the creativity of students' approaches to bring this point home. Comments such as the following show students that you value them coming up with unique solutions to problems, which in turn encourages them to take the intellectual risks necessary to become confident thinkers:

- I didn't think of this strategy!
- This is a clever use of factoring.
- This step reminds me of the example we looked at when _____.
- I like how you adapted the idea from _____ to solve this problem.

Feedback of this sort helps students see themselves as part of a broader community of mathematical thinkers. By referencing their chosen strategies and putting them into context, you help students link their creative ideas to the field of mathematics itself.

In a 2021 article for Edutopia, Alex Shevrin Venet writes about English teachers using positive comments to help students understand how their writing resonates with readers. As she notes, "Positive comments highlighting our reading experience can encourage students to think about their audience more intentionally as they write" (para. 7). Here are a few possible examples:

- You crafted _____ so smoothly by _____.
- You navigate this topic in such an engaging way, especially by _____.
- You chose the perfect tone for this topic by _____.
- When I read this, it reminded me of _____.

Celebrating Growth and Perseverance

Learning is challenging, and teachers play an essential role in encouraging students to persevere through difficult content. By recognizing students' progress and persistence, we can motivate them to push through future challenges. Here are some examples of feedback that celebrates growth and perseverance:

- Great job catching the mistake here.
- This was a long and complex process! By keeping your work organized and sticking to your plan, you persevered.

- I noticed you struggled with this skill last unit, but this line shows you've mastered it now! Excellent work staying committed.

Students may not notice their own growth, so pointing out specific instances can help them see that their hard work pays off.

Sparking Curiosity and Promoting Deeper Thinking

Positive feedback can drive students at all levels to explore beyond the content by sparking curiosity and promoting deeper thinking. Here are some examples of such feedback that I often use in math and that can be adapted across subject areas:

- What about this problem helped you realize this strategy was needed?
- How did you check your work?
- What strategies helped you keep track of all the steps?
- How will you remember the connection you made here?
- What might change if the problem were slightly different?

These questions reinforce the idea that learning doesn't end just because you've aced an exam. They encourage students to keep questioning, remain curious, and apply their knowledge in new ways. For example, when we ask, "What might change if the problem were slightly different?" students will have to not only extend their reasoning from this scenario to a different one but also imagine what other possible problems the particular skill they have just demonstrated allows them to unlock.

Ensuring That Feedback Is Constructive

To ensure that feedback is not only positive but also constructive, comments should focus on the skill students are developing rather than on the students themselves. Simple adjustments to your language allow you to do this. You can start by avoiding "you" phrases—for example, instead of "You need to work on transition sentences," say something like "Adding a transition sentence would help the flow of this paragraph into the next idea."

Another strategy is to make sure your comments refer back to something physical, such as a rubric or specific elements of the student's work. For example, instead of "You are too nervous during presentations," refer to a particular event and comment on specific, actionable body cues: "Think about the speech you gave last week and compare it to some of the great speeches that we watched together. Notice how all the strong speakers exuded so much confidence! They did this by standing up tall, projecting their voices loudly, and limiting the number of times they reference their cue cards." These specifics provide students with a goal for your next feedback conversation rather than making them feel like their skills are inadequate.

In addition to simple language shifts, consider employing feedback protocols that empower students. One such protocol is the Strengths, Needs, Next Steps approach suggested by Angela Di Michele Lalor (2022). First, identify what the student can do, which helps restore students' confidence in themselves as capable of learning. Then identify where the student needs to go to achieve the learning target. (Remember to be specific and avoid "you" statements.) Finally, make sure to include next steps that specify what the student needs to do to move forward with their learning. Differentiate and tailor these next steps to students' individual strengths and preferred learning styles.

Providing the Right Amount of Feedback and Ensuring That It's Timely

Have you ever had an essay turned back to you covered in red ink, with words crossed out and comments filling the margins? I certainly have, and it left me feeling like my paper was total junk. Rather than read the comments and address each one individually, my instinct was to toss the paper and start over. Luckily, I had a patient mom talk me down and help me respond rationally.

When we give students a ton of feedback all at once, we bombard them with their deficits, draining their confidence and detracting from their ability to focus on the specific skills you want them to work on. Instead, provide feedback in stages.

For example, if providing feedback on an essay, have students submit their papers multiple times, and then provide targeted feedback each time.

The first round can focus on structure, organization, and efficacy of supporting evidence; the second round on flow and word choice; and the third round on grammar and sentence structure. This way, the students are not overwhelmed and can prioritize what they need to work on.

I know a calculus teacher who always provides two types of feedback on his assessments. He uses one color pen to address the new skills and standards students are learning in class and a second color pen to focus on the skills students are already supposed to have mastered, such as basic algebraic computations. By distinguishing the feedback in this way, students don't just see a wrong answer, they often felt validated because they understand the calculus concept even though they may have misremembered a rule from Algebra 2.

It is critical to make sure that feedback is timely. In other words, don't wait too long to provide it. We want students to feel comfortable taking risks in their learning, even if it means making errors, but we certainly do not want misconceptions to become engrained. The longer a student believes that a mistake is correct, the more difficult it is for them to redirect their neural pathways to the correct line of thinking.

Using Feedback as a Learning Opportunity

When we respond to an incorrect answer with "Can someone help him out?" or draw an X across a student's paper, we invalidate their response and move on from it. Instead, we should invite further discussion by digging into the student's thought process. Remember, the goal is to create an environment where students see mistakes as opportunities to learn and grow. By focusing on improvement and providing positive reinforcement, you can help students develop resilience and a positive attitude toward challenges.

Examples of Ineffective Versus Effective Feedback

The following are some examples of ineffective feedback along with counterexamples of feedback that helps reduce student anxiety about making mistakes.

"This Should Be Easy for You!"

Example: A teacher is introducing a lesson about substituting values for variables in an expression. Before presenting the concept to the class, the teacher says, "Today should be totally easy since you all understand the order of operations."

This example isn't exactly "feedback" on a student's work, but it is helpful for the student to see how they are supposed to interpret the content to come. Furthermore, it highlights language we often use as teachers. We might say something like, "This should be easy for you! You must be overthinking it." Alternatively, we might preface new content with "This is easy compared to what we did last week." What do you think students feel when they hear that something is supposed to be "easy"? Some might be relieved, but others might feel a crippling anxiety, since it means the teacher probably won't expect them to make mistakes.

Counterexample: The teacher introduces the topic by saying, "Today's topic builds on what you've been learning about order of operations. Though it might look new at first, I am confident you'll be able to make connections and apply what you already know in order to make progress."

"Can Someone Help Her Out?"

Example: In a science class, during a unit on density, a teacher asks, "If I drop a soccer ball and a bowling ball off the roof, which will fall faster?" One student quickly responds that the bowling ball will fall faster. The teacher responds, "Nope. Can someone help her out?"

The student feels both ashamed and confused—ashamed to have answered so confidently only to be told that she's wrong in front of her classmates, and confused that her previous learning didn't help her answer the question correctly.

Counterexample: The teacher responds, "Can you explain why you think that?" The student points out that the bowling ball is denser than the soccer ball so it will "sink" through the air more readily. The teacher acknowledges the student's awareness of density and validates her logic, then explains why this situation is different.

"I Don't Think You Understand."

Example: A student's essay for English class has a strong introduction and outline but poorly developed body paragraphs. The teacher does not comment on the introduction or organization but makes a lot of negative comments throughout the body of the text. For example, "You haven't connected this quote to the main idea of this paragraph" and "I don't think you understand how to properly write citations." In several places, the teacher has circled an entire sentence and simply written "grammar" next to it.

Counterexample: Instead of just writing "grammar" next to a circled sentence, the teacher explains the errors she sees and the skills the student needs to learn to correct them. The teacher also leaves comments that praise what the student has done well and emphasize learning opportunities over student flaws:

- I can tell that you really worked hard and incorporated the previous feedback you received on your introduction. This paragraph draws me in and gives me a clear and organized understanding of the direction your paper is headed.

- This is a good quote, but I'm not sure how it relates to the main idea of the paragraph. Providing a few more explanatory sentences to make that connection for the reader would make the quote more effective.

- Let's work together on citation strategies. Here is an example of a properly cited quote and the accompanying entry in the Works Cited. Try to follow the example to correct the other citations, and we'll go over them together.

Auditing Your Own Feedback

Consider auditing your own feedback. Look at a stack of papers that you recently graded or film a lesson and then review it using a chart like the one in Figure 3.1.

Figure 3.1

Feedback Auditing Form Template

Student Mistake	Original Feedback	Revised Feedback

FAQs

Q: If my feedback is primarily positive, how will my students know that they are wrong? Will I instill a false sense of confidence?

A: Positive feedback should always be constructive and make students aware of areas where they need to redouble their learning. It also *should* instill a sense of confidence in students that they can improve.

Q: How can I find the time to provide such detailed feedback? It's more efficient to just tell them what's wrong.

A: It may be faster to tell students that they're wrong than go to the trouble of providing more detailed feedback, but simply pointing out flaws will only lead to wasted time down the road. If students don't learn how to do things correctly, you might end up having to give the same feedback over and over again. Students may also become more reserved and less confident, making them less likely to participate in class. They may take longer to learn the material because they are too afraid of being wrong to actively engage with it.

Conclusion

This chapter illustrates how encouraging, positive feedback cultivates students' self-confidence, curiosity, and willingness to take intellectual risks. Effective feedback highlights students' strengths, guides them to reflect on their reasoning, and addresses specific skills rather than personal flaws. Constructive feedback that focuses on learning growth promotes resilience and improvement without overwhelming students. By balancing positive reinforcement with clear, skill-based constructive feedback, teachers can create a classroom culture that values effort, celebrates progress, and builds a foundation for lifelong learning and self-efficacy.

In the next chapter, we'll consider another way to regularly promote mistake-making in class: by having students play guessing games and engage in prediction activities.

Additional Resources

- The full text of Alex Shevrin Venet's Edutopia article "How to Give Positive Feedback on Student Writing" can be found at www.edutopia.org/article/how-give-positive-feedback-student -writing.

- I also wrote an article for Edutopia, inspired by Shevrin Venet's and applying her ideas to math classrooms. You can find it at www.edutopia.org/article/using-positive-feedback-math-classrooms.

4

Guessing Games and Prediction Activities

"How many eggs do you suppose the average American eats in a year?" When I posed this prompt to my students, they responded with questions of their own:

- "Does it have to be an actual egg, or are we counting eggs that are baked into food like brownies?"
- "Are there eggs in bread?"
- "How much do eggs cost?"
- "How many eggs have I eaten today?"

The class discussed, joked with one another, and, eventually, each one made a guess. One of my vegan students guessed 50. An athlete, using their own experience as a reference, guessed 1,000. The truth? In 2023, the average American ate 281 eggs (Shahbandeh, 2024). None of my students was egg-zactly right (sorry), yet none was embarrassed by their incorrect answers, either—they had grown accustomed to being "wrong" on this kind of activity since I regularly used it in class.

I didn't choose the egg prompt because it was somehow related to the calculus content we would be studying that day. In fact, I chose it partly because it *wasn't* related to the day's content. I had a daily desk calendar with a random statistic on it for each day of the year, and we steadily worked through them, one day at a time. We built a routine out of starting every class with a guessing game where nobody had the expectation of being right. Doing so allowed my students to relax, smile, build trust in me and in one another, and get themselves in a good headspace to take chances with their learning that day.

Here's another example of how effective guessing games like this are at engaging students. One day in 2023, I needed a substitute to cover my class. When I returned to the room the next morning, I looked at my whiteboard and smiled. A student had written the following prompt: "How much does a blue whale's heart weigh?" He had looked up the prompt and answer on his own, written it on the board, and facilitated the guessing activity with the class. He had even gotten the substitute to participate!

Over the next two days, this student asked to continue facilitating our daily guessing game. He wanted to stick with the theme, so his next two prompts were "How much does a blue whale's brain weigh?" and "How much does a blue whale's tongue weigh?" On those days, I participated as a guesser. At first, I was nervous; as the teacher, I felt I should be able to answer my student's question. In the end, I didn't even have the closest guess that day, and you know what? It was fine! We all laughed about our guesses, and on the second day, I was totally comfortable venturing an estimate along with the class. I had felt firsthand the positive effect that this activity had on mistake culture.

According to Merriam-Webster (2004), *to guess* means "to form an opinion from little or no evidence." This definition suggests that when we invite students to make a guess, we shouldn't expect them to know the correct answer. Instead, we want to invoke a sense of whimsy and keep the stakes low. Teachers can accomplish this by prompting their students in such a way that the only factor determining whether they've guessed correctly is random chance.

In this chapter, we discuss two different ways to incorporate guessing into your classroom: by playing silly guessing games that have little to do with the content students are learning and by aligning prediction activities to course content. Both strategies help students become accustomed to being wrong in a low-stress environment and provide additional benefits to learning.

Criteria for Effective Guessing Games

The more we practice making mistakes, the more comfortable we become with them. I remember being so terrified of making a mistake during my first week of teaching that I was sick to my stomach before every lesson regardless of how prepared I was. By the end of the week, the sickness had gone away and I'd found that I could be myself with my students. Externally, nothing had changed, yet my body and brain learned that I was safe in this new and unfamiliar setting.

When we have opportunities to practice something we fear and see that it doesn't end in catastrophe, we start to unlearn that fear. Unfortunately, even though just one or two negative experiences can cause us to develop a fear, many repeated positive experiences are needed to unlearn it. For example, if you get into a single bad accident while skiing, it might take many safe encounters with skis for you to overcome your fear. The good news is that safe exposure and habituation, especially when it is frequent and within a short time window, is an effective way to unlearn fear (Cain et al., 2003; Marks & Tobeña, 1990).

To effectively alleviate students' fear of making mistakes, classroom guessing games should conform to the following criteria:

- Student guesses should not be graded or judged in any way.
- All students should have a roughly equal chance of guessing correctly.
- The games should be regularly implemented in class.
- The games should encourage participation from all students.

Student Guesses Should Not Be Graded or Judged in Any Way

This criterion is necessary to ensure that students don't feel punished for making a mistake. Students should not be judged on their guesses or made to feel that being wrong indicates a flaw in them as learners or humans. Detaching grades from guesses ensures that students don't feel pressured to be right or fear encountering a negative consequence if they're wrong. If students ask whether a guessing game is graded, you can say something along these lines: "This game won't be graded, but it still has value. It helps you become comfortable with not being correct all the time."

All Students Should Have a Roughly Equal Chance of Guessing Correctly

One way to ensure that no student has an edge over the others in a guessing game is by selecting silly or improbable prompts that do not rely on prior knowledge. For example, when we ask, "How many dimples does a golf ball have?" students are likely on an equal playing field. However, if we ask, "How many protons are there in a carbon atom?" students may feel pressure to know this because it is something that some of them may have learned in chemistry class. When all students feel that they are on an equal playing field, they feel less embarrassed when they guess incorrectly. Humor relaxes tensions and makes learning more comfortable; as one student put it, "The classes in which I succeed most are the ones where teachers are very funny, where we can make mistakes" (The Learning Network, 2019). Figure 4.1 shows examples of prompts that don't meet this criterion and possible ways to rework them.

The Games Should Be Regularly Implemented in Class

Getting over a fear requires repeated confirmation that when the thing you fear occurs, it does not result in the negative outcome you anticipated. If students are not exposed to consequence-free mistake-making enough times, or if the interval between exposures is too long, they won't overcome the fear for a sustained period of time (Cain et al., 2003; Marks & Tobeña, 1990).

Figure 4.1

Examples of and Revisions to Unfair Guessing Game Prompts

Unfair Prompt	Why It's Unfair	Possible Revision	Why the Revision Is Better
How many Grammy awards has Taylor Swift won?	This is a pop culture question that might have some students feeling left out. True "Swifties" will know the actual answer and not even need to guess.	How long is the average pop song?	The revised prompt is still related to pop music, but it isn't as narrow and lets all students draw on prior experience.
Michelangelo's David was originally modeled after which hero of myth?	Students with domain knowledge about myth or art will have an edge here. This prompt also feels overly academic.	[Teacher shows an image of an obscure work of art and asks students to guess the title.]	The revised prompt has no single right answer and allows students to use their creativity.
What is the most popular Thanksgiving side dish?	This question is specific to U.S. culture. Some students may not have ever experienced a Thanksgiving dinner.	[Teacher shows a picture of a Thanksgiving turkey.] How much do you think this turkey weighed when it was still alive?	The revised prompt gives students necessary context to make a guess.

The Games Should Encourage Participation from All Students

Keeping guessing games low-stakes and fun makes it likelier that all students will want to participate in them. If they don't, you can gently encourage them to take a chance and remind them that you don't expect them to be right. In my own class, there were days when one or two students wouldn't want to play until their classmates began to cheer them on, reassuring them that it was all just for fun.

Prediction Activities Aligned to Course Content

Prediction activities aligned to course content are meant to take advantage of the learning benefits of being wrong. When students make an incorrect guess, they recognize a gap in their knowledge and are inspired to fill it, which helps with content retention.

In my precalculus class, I used a prediction activity to help students understand how to determine certain features of a graph from the algebraic expression of a function. One of my students reflected, "I remembered the rules so much better because I had figured them out on my own by guessing the pattern."

Prediction Activity in Action

Social studies teacher Scott Roberts designed a prediction activity to inspire his students to think deeply about the impact of the Articles of Confederation on the drafting of the U.S. Constitution. He knew that his students had not yet made the historical connection between the two documents, so they would truly be guessing the outcome.

Roberts's first step was to carefully curate resources that allowed students to explore the Articles of Confederation but did not address their influence on the Constitution. Students read through the resources and drew their own conclusions about the weaknesses of the Articles of Confederation.

Next, Roberts split students into groups and assigned one of the weaknesses of the Articles to each team. He prompted them to predict how they thought the Framers had used the Articles to write the Constitution. Then he revealed the surprising truth that they had actually thrown out the Articles and started from scratch!

Students then compared their predictions about what really happened. As Roberts (2016) himself put it, "In this step, students could determine how their ideas agreed with or differed from those of the Framers, some of America's most famous historical figures. Students became excited as they discovered similarities, such as 'my idea was just like the Virginia Plan'" (p. 48).

This example might not fit your context perfectly, but I hope it can still inspire you to think about how you might use content-aligned prediction activities in your own class. The key is to follow the flow of the lesson plan:

1. Identify a concept you want your students to think critically about but they haven't been taught yet.
2. Give students enough tools to explore and build a base of knowledge about the concept.
3. Prompt them to make a prediction about something related to the concept that wasn't addressed in their learning.
4. Reveal the real answer.
5. Have students compare their predictions to the real answer.

Use the template in Figure 4.2 to plan an upcoming lesson using this strategy.

Figure 4.2

Prediction Activity Planning Template

Concept:

Resources or examples that provide necessary context or background knowledge:

-
-
-
-

Prediction prompt:

Answer to the prompt and description of how you will reveal it to students:

Here are a few example prompts for content-aligned prediction activities across subject areas that are designed to follow the lesson flow:

- **Math:** Provide students with examples and nonexamples of parallelograms and ask them to come up with a definition of a parallelogram and a list of its properties.

- **Science:** Show students a picture of a Rube Goldberg machine where a marble can end up in one of several different locations. Ask students to predict where the marble will end up.

- **English language arts:** Read the introductory paragraph of a literary essay and predict what the main ideas of the next three supporting paragraphs will be.

A natural time to implement an activity such as this is on the first day of a new unit, either in combination with or as an alternative to pretesting, giving an introductory lecture, showing a video, or using a KWL chart.

Prediction Activities Tangential to Content Area

Prediction activities don't have to address course content to help students shed their anxiety about mistake-making. Consider starting class every day by providing students with a prompt that requires a quick answer: a number, a name, a place, a single sentence. This activity is not meant to take very much class time, and answers shouldn't be too involved. The prompt should be tangentially related to the class content area but should not address material you might ask about on a formal assessment. Keeping the prompt disconnected from the current learning ensures that the activity doesn't feel like a quiz. Here are some examples:

- **Math:** Have students use Three Act Math to tap into their number sense. The first act typically shows an image or a video and asks students to use math to make a prediction about the scenario. The second act adds numbers to the original prompt and asks students to refine their prediction. The answer is revealed in the third act.

- **English language arts:** Present students with a sentence from a famous novel or poem that has a word missing and ask them to predict what word it is.

- **Social studies:** Show students a picture of a building or landscape and ask students to guess the location.

- **Science:** Show students a photo of something magnified to a microscopic degree and ask them to guess what it is.

- **World languages:** Show students a word in the language being studied and ask them to guess the meaning.

Present the prompt and allow students a minute or two of thinking time. This is my favorite part because lively discussions and curious questions often result as students think through the prompt. Then write all the answers on the board and show appreciation for each one. Point out some of the more interesting guesses before revealing the correct answer.

This activity follows the same flow as the first type but differs in several ways. Since it is not related to content, it lowers the stakes even further. It also occurs much more frequently and is therefore even more effective in helping students diminish the fear response. It's easy to fit into your daily routine and doesn't require you to rewrite any lesson plans. In fact, I use the activity to take attendance because I can easily see who isn't in class by identifying who did not make guesses!

FAQs

Q: Can I grade these activities?

A: Most schools require teachers to enter grades regularly. If you feel the pressure to assign a grade to every class activity or if you feel that a participation grade is necessary to encourage students to engage in guessing games and prediction activities, there is room for compromise here. Ideally, grades should be an accurate reflection of what students know and are able to do with the academic content of your course. They should not be used to control student behaviors.

With that in mind, I think it would still be possible to assign grades at least to the content-aligned prediction activities outlined in this chapter.

I would not grade the actual prediction students make, since it would be unfair to penalize them for being wrong. However, if you have them analyze the differences between what they predicted and the reality, their analysis could fairly be assigned a formative assessment grade. Note, you are still not grading the prediction itself. You are grading the analysis of it.

For example, suppose you're a physics teacher and you asked your students to predict where a tennis ball would land given the projection angle and speed. Chances are that without understanding projectile motions, students' guesses will be far from accurate. It would be unfair to grade them based on their gut instincts. However, at the end of the unit, students could perform the calculation to determine the correct result and compare it to their intuitive guesses for a grade. Again, you are not grading the prediction but rather the learning that has happened since then.

Q. How do you ensure that students remain engaged in these guessing games over time, rather than seeing them as repetitive or unimportant?

A: To ensure that students remain engaged in guessing games over time, variety and student involvement are key. Here are some strategies:

- **Use unexpected or thematic prompts.** Keep the prompts fresh and surprising. You might tie them to current events, pop culture, or holidays. For example, around Halloween, you could ask, "How many pounds of candy corn are sold each year?"

- **Let students take ownership.** Encourage students to bring in their own guessing prompts, as seen in the example of the student who led the whale heart activity. When students create and facilitate the game, they feel a sense of investment and excitement.

- **Gamify the experience.** Even though the activity isn't graded, you can add friendly competition by tracking "most creative guesses" or "closest estimates" in a lighthearted way. Rotating small rewards (such as letting the winner choose the next question) can also boost engagement.

- **Encourage humor and playfulness.** The more lighthearted and fun the atmosphere, the more likely students will look forward to participating. Acknowledging creative or funny answers helps reinforce the idea that there's no pressure to be right.

By maintaining novelty, encouraging student-led participation, and keeping the environment fun and relaxed, you can sustain student engagement and ensure that guessing games remain an enjoyable and beneficial part of the learning experience.

Conclusion

In this chapter, we explored ways to design guessing and predicting opportunities to help students become comfortable sharing "wrong" answers. To effectively calm students' fears of making a mistake, prompts should be practically impossible to answer correctly, and activities should be used on a regular basis. We also addressed content-aligned prediction activities, which ask students to make guesses about topics you'll be covering in class and then revisit those initial ideas throughout the learning process. In the next chapter, we'll turn the power of design over to students. By reflecting on content, they will write their own content-related questions and intentionally generate "wrong" answers for their classmates to analyze.

Additional Resources

- To read about Scott Roberts's lesson on the Articles of Confederation in more detail, check out his article "Keep 'Em Guessing: Using Student Predictions to Inform Historical Understanding and Empathy" in *Social Studies Research and Practice*.

- I love the KidsKonnect article "13 Fun and Educational Guessing Games for Kids," which you can find here: https://kidskonnect .com/articles/guessing-games-for-kids. The article discusses game ideas and the associated learning benefits in reading, writing, and math.

- For a great discussion of normalizing failure that touches on many of the points made in this chapter, check out episode 90 of E. Scott England's *Anchored in Education* podcast.

5

Collaborative
Mistake Analysis

Mistake analysis is a strategy that has grown in popularity across classrooms, and for good reason. As I note in the Introduction, thinking metacognitively about errors is the critical step in transforming a mistake into a learning experience. Analyzing errors is a way to structure metacognitive reflection and promote learning.

The basic structure for mistake analysis is to present an example of incorrect work to students and ask them to identify any errors they see. For each error they identify, students explain what makes it a mistake. Diagnosing errors in this way draws students' attention to common misconceptions and gives them strategies for assessing the correctness of their own work.

There are many ways to enhance the basic structure of this activity for greater effectiveness. For example, consider following the identification of errors with a conversation about more efficient strategies for achieving the task (Palincsar & Brown, 1984; Rushton, 2018). In fact, mistake analysis is most effective when the error is compared to correct examples

(Santagata, 2005). When students compare a mistake to the right way of doing something, they learn to associate mistake-making with learning. This process, called recursive reminding, ensures that when students recall the error, they will also recall how to correct it (Jacoby & Wahlheim, 2013).

Mistake analysis is also more effective when students themselves generate the mistakes they analyze, whether intentionally or not. Often, when students make errors, they genuinely believe their answers to be true—this allows them to analyze the thinking that went into making the error so they can correct it. A teacher who generates an error and presents it to the class for analysis fails to take advantage of students' existing mental schema, and the activity may end up distracting them rather than serving as a learning opportunity (Metcalfe, 2017).

The following is an example of my favorite way to use mistake analysis for promoting learning in the classroom.

Activity in Action

I smiled as I surveyed the room. Students in each group were in heated discussion about the mistakes they had made over the previous two weeks of our unit about taking the derivatives of functions. One group wrote an example in which the wrong rule was applied. Another group chose the correct rule but included a computational error. A third group generated a complicated function that required a different, more complicated rule but left out a step in the application.

The students in each group intentionally generated mistakes by drawing from their own experiences with the content. As they moved around the room, they studied the mistakes generated by their classmates, often saying things like, "Oh! I've made that mistake before! I know what to do!"

When I met with each student individually for our end-of-unit assessment conferences, I asked them to describe aspects of the unit that were difficult for them as well as anything that helped them overcome those challenges. Many reflected on the value of this mistake-analysis exercise.

"At first, I kept trying to use the power rule when I really needed to use the rule for exponential functions," said one student. "After we did the mistake activity, I started to be more on the lookout for these functions and I remembered which rule to use." Another student said, "I used to always forget that the derivative of a constant is zero, but when we high-lighted that mistake at the board, I started to be able to correct myself before messing up."

I typically designate a full class period to the activity so I can provide students with plenty of processing time and possibly go through more than one cycle. The length of each round depends on the complexity of the topic you are reviewing and on how involved you want the examples students generate to be.

Preparation

The first step is to split the class into groups of three or four. Use a grouping strategy that you and your students are comfortable with. (I typically group students randomly using a random number generator.) Assign each group to an area of the room equipped with either a white-board or poster paper taped to the wall. One of the beautiful aspects of this activity is that it gets students up and moving around, adding a buzz of energy to the space.

Notify students that their groups will participate in three rounds of collaboration and that they need to identify a different scribe for each round. The scribe will be the only person allowed to hold the marker during that round so all other participants must clearly share their ideas with one another and agree on what the scribe should write.

Round 1

Once students are in their designated locations, provide a prompt along these lines:

Generate a problem similar to ones you've been working on, and provide an incorrect solution to it.

Guide students to recall an error they have made or seen their class-mates make. Explain that they are not to identify the error, simply to solve the problem incorrectly. Here are some examples of ways students might approach this activity in different content areas:

- **Math:** solving a math equation incorrectly
- **English language arts:** writing a paragraph riddled with grammatical mistakes
- **Social studies:** incorrectly interpreting a primary source document
- **Science:** creating a diagram of a process that misrepresents one of the stages

I once used this activity in a prealgebra class during a unit on adding and subtracting fractions. One group came up with example $\frac{5}{6} + \frac{4}{7} = \frac{9}{13}$ because some of their group members had made the mistake of not getting a common denominator before adding. Another group used the example $\frac{3}{5} + \frac{5}{7} = \frac{3}{7}$, demonstrating an improper use of the "canceling out" that occurs when we multiply two fractions. Metacognitive reflection really kicks in as students discuss the mistakes they have made, almost made, or seen others make. If they are struggling to generate examples, allow them to look back at previous assignments to prompt their thinking. As my students worked on their examples, they thought about areas in problem sets they had worked on and bell-ringer activities from the previous week that had confused them.

Before moving on to Round 2, make sure that when each group writes down its problem and incorrect solution, the error isn't somehow identified.

Round 2

Once each group has written out its problem and incorrect solution, have students rotate so that each group is in front of another group's problem. Provide the second prompt:

In this round, your group will analyze the work done by a different group. Identify the error in the work but do not correct it. Instead, use a different color to correctly respond to the same problem right next to the incorrect version.

Here, students move beyond metacognitive reflection to consider alternative effective solutions. It is during this part of the activity that correct processes are engrained and coded into memory alongside common misconceptions. Make sure students don't simply edit the incorrect problem but rewrite it correctly in full. (It's OK if the response they produce in this round is unintentionally incorrect. If this is the case, it will be identified and corrected in the third and final round.)

Round 3

Each group rotates again so that now they are looking at both an intentionally incorrectly solved problem and a rewritten version intended to be correct. The prompt for this round should be as follows:

> In this round, your group should study the two previous groups' responses. Your job is to interpret the original mistake. Answer these questions: "What was this group's thought process as they made this mistake? Why might they have thought it was correct?" Then check the correct response. First, make sure that it is in fact correct. Then explain why it is more effective than the original response.

Students do the important work of comparing a correct response to an incorrect response during this round. By analyzing the thought patterns that could lead someone to make the mistake, they clarify how the misconception took root. After providing processing time, gather the whole class for a gallery walk and share-out at each paper or whiteboard. Allow each group to explain the work they did during Round 3 to the rest of the class.

Benefits of Mistake Analysis

There are a slew of benefits to the activity shared in this chapter. My favorite is that students must do several different types of thinking. Having students generate examples of common misconceptions requires them to engage deeply in metacognitive reflection. Identifying and articulating an error involves precise critical analysis of the steps involved, which reinforces students' understanding of the content. As they work to correct the mistake, they hone their problem-solving skills. Finally, explaining a solution from another's perspective requires them to develop a well-structured argument.

Another benefit of the activity is that it provides an accessible entry point for every student. Those who struggle can reflect on mistakes they've made on past assignments, whereas advanced students can explore subtler errors that might challenge their peers. The collaborative approach fosters teamwork and ensures that every student has a way to contribute. Even those facing the greatest difficulties can share the types of problems they find most challenging and reflect on errors they've encountered. What's more, having only one student handle the writing per round ensures that each group member contributes actively. The other members need to communicate to their scribe, and everyone needs to agree before anything is written down.

The dynamic, multistep nature of this activity generates palpable energy in the classroom. There's an exciting buzz as students move around the board, brainstorming, debating, and shifting their focus. Personally, I've always believed that standing up and writing on a large surface enhances our thinking.

This activity can be applied at various stages of the learning process. Early on, it helps correct misconceptions before they become engrained. In the middle of a unit, it encourages students to pause and reflect on their mistakes before they become habitual. The activity is also valuable as a review or preparation for summative assessment at the end of a unit. However, I wouldn't recommend using this strategy to introduce new content—it works best when students have some familiarity with the material and have had a chance to practice and receive feedback first.

FAQs

Q: Doesn't having students come up with mistakes reinforce mistake-making rather than mitigate it?

A: This is a common concern. Some teachers also fear that students might confuse the correct and incorrect responses when recalling the activity. Although these fears are reasonable, research has shown them to be unfounded (Pillai et al., 2020). Time and again, studies show the value of mistake analysis to learning, especially when mistakes are scrutinized alongside correct solutions (Cyr & Anderson, 2018; Kawasaki, 2010).

Q: Will sharing mistakes with peers harm students' egos?

A: The beauty of this activity is that students don't need to own up to actually having made the mistake! They can recognize that a mistake is common and note that they have seen it made before without sharing that they have made it themselves. In conversations during this activity, I have heard students say things like, "I could imagine someone messing this up like this." At the same time, recognizing the ubiquity of mistakes is an important aspect of building a healthier mistake culture in the room. This activity accomplishes that goal without students risking embarrassment in front of their peers.

Q: How do I manage this strategy with a large class or with students who are too quiet or timid to get involved?

A: Some teachers with large class sizes may be concerned about there being too many groups to observe or too many students in a group. Quiet students may be left out of the activity. Of course this is a potential challenge.

Amber Riel is just one of many teachers who have found success with the activity in a class as large as 30 students. Amber allots three students to each group and gives each student in the group a different-colored marker. She makes sure to look for all three colors on the board and to backtrack and use direct instruction if students are not following along, to consolidate learning at the end of the lesson, or when all students get stuck at the same spot. "It usually requires five minutes or less of a huddle and then release to continue working," she notes (personal communication).

There will always be timid students in classrooms, but there are ways you can encourage every student to participate. For example, if I'm concerned that some students are dominating the discussion and others are lacking understanding, I will announce in Round 3 that I intend to randomly choose one group member to share on behalf of the whole group. This motivates everyone to ask the questions that they need to in order to understand the work and report out.

Q: Can I use this activity in an asynchronous online setting?

A: It is definitely possible to adapt this strategy for asynchronous and online classrooms, though you may lose the group-work component. My suggestion would be to create a collaborative shared document with one blank page per student. Label each page with a number and assign each student to a numbered page. In Round 1, have each student choose a color in which to write their incorrectly solved problem. In Round 2, they scroll to the next numbered page and analyze the work there, using a different color to rewrite the problem correctly alongside the original. In Round 3, students move to the next page and analyze the work and thought patterns of the previous two students who were there. They either write their analysis below the previous students' work in a third color or record a short screencast explaining their discoveries.

Conclusion

This chapter focused on the educational benefits of mistake analysis, which encourages students to learn from errors by actively reflecting on and diagnosing them. The activity presented in the chapter involves students working in groups to create intentional mistakes based on common misconceptions they or their classmates have encountered. Other groups then identify and correct these mistakes, reinforcing understanding through metacognitive reflection and collaborative problem-solving. This activity is especially effective when students generate their own mistakes and helps embed correct approaches to problems by having them compare errors to correct answers. The three-round format encourages the development of critical thinking and error-recognition skills and is adaptable across subjects and class sizes.

In the next chapter, we'll explore a more common application of mistake analysis in which the entire class works together to analyze one mistake at a time rather than working in small groups.

Additional Resources

- I first wrote about the mistake-analysis activity in this chapter for Edutopia. You can read the article here: www.edutopia.org/article /collaborative-approach-mistake-analysis

- Edutopia's Facebook page has several threads where community members share their questions about and positive experiences with the activity. Here is one such thread: www.facebook.com/share /p/1UcVwY2bRF

- Don Marlett's learning-focused article "Learning Through Mistakes: How Deliberate Errors Can Boost Student Engagement and Retention" explains how deliberately making errors and correcting them while taking notes improves learning. You can read the article here: https://learningfocused.com/learning-through-mistakes-how -deliberate-errors-can-boost-student-engagement-and-retention

6

Analyzing the Mistakes of Former Students

In my first year teaching boarding school, I made a critical mistake. Another teacher and I had taken students on an overnight camping trip over the weekend. We had prepared for the trip well. The day before, we gathered sleeping bags, camping supplies, plenty of food, and fixings for s'mores, and we stopped by the wellness center to pick up medications prescribed to the students who had signed up for the trip. The morning of the trip, several students chose to stay on campus (or slept in) instead of joining us to camp. This left us with extra medications. My colleague and I decided to throw away the extra meds. I can't remember what led to the decision, but I would soon regret it.

Upon returning to campus, we were told that there were a slew of reasons why we should not have thrown away the extra medications. We were asked to fill out an official incident report the school would hold onto, which would be added to our professional files. I was horrified, embarrassed, and worried about any potential consequences of this error. To make matters worse, during the next faculty meeting, the nurse made an announcement to the whole faculty about the incident. She didn't share our names, only referring to us as anonymous teachers, and though she intended to use our mistake as an opportunity to remind everyone else of proper protocols, it also served to scar me deeply. In my 10 years at the school, my relationship with the nurse was strained.

Mistakes *are* valuable learning opportunities. I certainly learned my lesson and will never again think lightly about how I handle unused medication. However, when our mistakes are raw and shared broadly among our peers, our sense of shame can be amplified, even if they are shared anonymously. When someone else shares a mistake that we made, we might shut down and close ourselves in. At the same time, mistakes are most valuable to learning when they are common, realistic, and relatable— the sorts of mistakes our peers make or that we make ourselves. This chapter presents a protocol for mistake analysis like the one in the previous chapter but with an additional safeguard for preventing student embarrassment: the mistakes analyzed belong to former rather than current students. Note that this activity works best if you have a preexisting archive of student work, but we will also discuss ways to modify it if you haven't gathered such a collection.

"My Favorite No"

The mistake-analysis protocol highlighted here is a variation on "My Favorite No," an activity popularized by the Teaching Channel (Midwinter, 2014). Before we discuss this protocol, here's how the original activity works. First, the teacher gives students a sample question to answer at the start of class, which each student answers on an index card. The teacher then collects all the index cards and quickly sorts the right answers from the wrong ones. Next, the teacher selects a wrong answer they find particularly interesting, thought-provoking, or representative of a common error. The teacher writes the wrong answer on the board for the class to analyze.

Students begin their analysis by stating what is *right* about the answer; they describe everything the student did correctly and well. Next, they discuss what went wrong, identifying the error(s). Finally, they conclude the analysis by discussing what the student might have been thinking that led them astray. As in the previous chapter, examining the thought process behind the error is critical.

This activity mitigates potential student embarrassment and anxiety in a couple of ways. First, it is ungraded, so the stakes are low. Second, the answers are anonymous and nobody can see the original handwriting to identify the student who made the chosen mistake. Third, the class begins by identifying everything that the student did correctly, helping to build their confidence. Finally, the activity shows them how common errors are and how natural it is for us to make them.

"Kids really love to do error analysis," says one middle school educator in the Bronx. "When you do it in class, students are actively engaged and thinking about the process." She added that students learn even more by being exposed to a variety of other people's errors than if they simply analyze their own.

Implementing the Activity

Though this activity can take as little as 15 minutes, the benefits it yields will be immense. It can serve as a formative assessment by asking about something you just taught that day or that week, as a diagnostic assessment by hinting at what you'll teach next, or as a spiral review by touching on a topic from a unit much earlier in the year.

The day before implementing the activity, conclude class with an exit-ticket prompt. The prompt should be complex enough that even if a student answers incorrectly, there is space for them to demonstrate some thinking that might be correct. In other words, the response to the prompt should not be limited to a single word. For example, rather than asking, "Where is DNA stored in a cell?" ask, "What is the function of the nucleus in a cell?" The latter requires a longer response that can more easily be analyzed. Since the former requires only a single-word answer, a student could respond, "Mitochondria," and the rest of the class would not have good insight into where that error came from. Each student answers the prompt and turns in their response before leaving class. This allows you to sort through the responses without using class time.

As you review the responses, look for common misconceptions or particularly instructive errors. Make copies of examples and save them to use with a different class down the road. Then go to an archive of previous answers to the same prompt and select a response from a former student that mirrors the kind of error you wish to highlight with your current students.

The next day in class, write the prompt and erroneous response you chose on the board. Have students begin by breaking down the response and identifying everything the student did correctly. They can also discuss anything they find interesting or creative about the response. (Students are almost always able to find at least two or three things that the response does well.) Students then identify the error and account for it. Solving the problem accurately is critical because it allows students to contrast the error with the correct answer, reinforcing the neural pathway for avoiding the mistake.

Finally, the class discusses the thought process behind the original response. This final discussion is the most exciting and my personal favorite part. It's fun to hear what the students identify as possible reasons for incorrect logic. When I first did this activity, I thought students might cop out and say something like "It's just a careless error." Instead, they said things like "They forgot their integer rules about negative numbers" or "They thought they could use the power rule, but the exponent has the variable so that rule doesn't actually apply here." When students have textured responses like these, I know they are reflecting on their own logic and mistakes in thinking rather than just what they see presented in front of them.

Here's an example. In my prealgebra class, we used this activity to examine combining like terms. I chose prompts where the solutions would involve multiple steps so there would be many opportunities for errors worth analyzing.

Simplify: $3(2x+1) - 2(2x-4)$

Here's the correct way to solve this:

Distribute: $6x + 3 - 4x + 8$

Combine like terms: $2x + 11$

The incorrect answer I shared with the class looked like this:

Parentheses: 3(3) – 2(–2)

Simplify: 9 – 4

This student made two mistakes. In the first step, they combined variable x terms with constant terms. In the second step, they multiplied two negative numbers and got a negative number.

During our discussion, the first student who spoke up said, "I think it should be + 4 in the second step."

Another student piped up, "That's true, but that step shouldn't even be there! Where did the x's go?"

The first student said, "Oh, yeah, you're right. They aren't supposed to mix $2x$ and 1."

A third student joined in, "I've made this mistake before, too! They can't combine $2x$ and 1! They need to distribute first!"

It was a great discussion and review of order of operations, integer rules, and combining like terms. I could feel the sense of community building as the students noticed their common ways of thinking.

Even though my example comes from a math class, the protocol can be used across subject areas. For example, in a history class, the prompt might be a short-answer question such as "What were three causes of the Revolutionary War?" The teacher would choose a response that displays reasonable logic but has a fundamental flaw or makes a common misconception. Discussing these common misconceptions leads to a richer understanding of the true causes of the war.

In adapting this activity to subject areas outside math, the critical part is understanding the common errors and misconceptions in your subject area and designing prompts that elicit those errors from students. Earlier in this chapter, I mentioned using this activity to review grammar in an English class, but it can also be used for spelling or vocabulary, to analyze paragraph structure, or to identify themes. Likewise, social studies teachers could prompt students to put events in chronological order. Any type of prompt that would elicit discussion-worthy mistakes is valid for mistake analysis.

FAQs

Q: How can I do this activity if I don't have a bank of former student responses?

A: If you don't have previous student responses, use the work of your current students—just make sure to write their answers on the board yourself. Alternatively, if you teach the same class to different groups of students, use work from a student in a different period. You might still want to write it on the board yourself so students can't possibly recognize handwriting. You may also want to ask the student for permission to use their work. If you do, make sure to praise them for what they did right and let them know that other students made a similar mistake. This helps them see that their work is being used for learning purposes, not because it's wrong or because they are somehow worse than their classmates.

If you use the work of current students, start a folder on your computer reserved for mistake analysis. Create subfolders labeled with the skills you want students to review. Throughout the year, add prompts and student responses that you find interesting and that have common errors to these subfolders. To make searching easy, label each file according to the mistake rather than the student's name. Within a year, you'll be able to use the work of former students rather than current students and you'll continue to add to your bank each year that you use the activity.

Q: How often should I do this?

A: Use mistake analysis as often as you like! If you often find errors in student responses, it may be helpful to use the activity as a lesson starter each day. If this sounds like too much, you could use the activity only to discuss the most important skills or those that require the highest depth of knowledge.

Conclusion

This chapter highlights the transformative potential of mistake analysis when applied thoughtfully in the classroom. By analyzing the anonymized work of former students, teachers create a safe space for current students to critically examine errors without fear of judgment or embarrassment. This practice allows students to deepen their understanding of content through reflective discussion, rather than simply by memorizing correct answers. "My Favorite No" serves as a powerful example of this approach, encouraging students to see mistakes as integral to learning and growth. This strategy helps teachers foster a classroom culture that views errors not as personal failures but as valuable learning moments.

In the next chapter, we'll explore Mistake Journals—a way for students to regularly reflect upon and analyze their own mistakes.

Additional Resources

- You can watch a video about "My Favorite No" here: www.youtube .com/watch?app=desktop&v=srJWx7P6uLE. It's really helpful to see and hear teacher Andy Midwinter put the activity in action so you know what to expect before trying it yourself!
- Don Marlett's article "Teaching Students Error Analysis: A Pathway to Critical Thinking" includes examples of the activity across content areas: https://learningfocused.com/teaching-students-error -analysis-a-pathway-to-critical-thinking/#ELA

7

Mistake Journals

Throughout my life, I have always kept journals. When I was young, I simply recounted my day-to-day activities: swim practice, homework, social drama, and all the other things that were important to me at that stage in my life. As I grew older, I continued to write about things that were important to me, but I also began to reflect on bigger themes in my life. In grad school, I used journals to write about my research—questions I had and ideas for where to go next with it. I even used journals to record my training for rock climbing.

What all these journals have in common is this: when I look back at them, I learn something. I gain insight into the throughlines connecting a younger version of myself to my current self. I see patterns in my thinking over time, things that have always been true for me and ways that my understanding has evolved. I notice how one event or action ended up being the catalyst for something else.

Journals are an incredible way to release some of our memories without losing them forever. They help us develop deeper understanding through analysis of our past thinking. For these reasons and more, they can also help students learn about and better understand the mistakes they make in the classroom.

The Importance of Reflection for Learning

Reflection is a critical part of learning, and I bet you are already having your students engage in it. Consistent reflection on learning helps students develop the ability to assess their own comfort level with material, explain what they know and can do, and be cognizant of where they need help. As educator and author Starr Sackstein (2015) notes, "Since I started using reflection with my students, I've witnessed profound growth in their ability to discuss their learning. They understand themselves as learners and often develop strategies for working to their own strengths and weaknesses. They are capable of asking for help in ways they couldn't before, making them advocates for their own learning" (p. 1).

Sackstein's students felt these benefits as well. As one student said, reflection "allows me to look back on the process of actually planning and writing my assignments as well as being able to identify the skills I actually learned and took away from the project. Reflections make me think about the challenges I faced and teach me how to approach similar problems in other situations" (Sackstein, 2015, p. 1).

Teachers play a critical role in scaffolding the reflection process. We can make reflection more effective for students by

- Providing them with prompts to reflect on.
- Setting clear expectations for high-quality reflection.
- Modeling the reflective process ourselves and through student exemplars.

Reflecting on Mistakes

There are a few things you can do to help students reflect on their mistakes in such a way that they learn from them. One is to encourage a sense of gratitude and appreciation rather than dread and self-deprecation.

For example, teacher Jennifer Mangels (2023) has students "put a heart around the error as a reminder that mistakes are important to the learning process" (para. 3). By guiding students to mark their mistakes in a positive way, you reinforce the idea that these are opportunities for learning that are welcome in the classroom.

Categorizing Mistakes

Another strategy is to teach students how to classify their mistakes. Eduardo Briceño (2015) of Mindset Works uses a clear taxonomy of errors that is easy for students to understand. He divides them into the following four categories, with the first two offering the greatest opportunity for student learning:

1. **A-ha moment mistakes:** These are mistakes that lead to an unexpected outcome, which in turn illuminates the error and leads to a new realization. For example, a student asked to solve $|3 - 5|$ may confidently respond with -2, believing that they know how to find the difference between 3 and 5. However, upon finding their answer is incorrect, that student realizes they didn't know that the two bars on the outside of the expression meant something. They learn that they need to know more about what those bars mean in order to solve the problem correctly. To have students reflect on these kinds of mistakes, Briceño suggests asking, "What was unexpected? Why did that result occur? What went well and what didn't? Is there anything I could try differently next time?"

2. **Stretch mistakes:** These mistakes are the result of trying to do something that is beyond our current ability level. We don't know what we're doing yet, so of course we'll make mistakes when operating in this zone! Stretch mistakes are positive because they mean we are challenging ourselves to grow. Reflecting on stretch mistakes means asking, "What is it that I need to learn to do in order to achieve the new goal?"

3. **Sloppy mistakes:** These mistakes occur when we aren't paying careful attention. By reflecting on what led us to a sloppy mistake (a bad night's sleep, chatting with a neighbor while working,

listening to music too loudly), we can better understand the conditions under which we perform best.

4. **High-stakes mistakes:** These are the mistakes that have the greatest potential consequences, such as on the SAT or a big unit test. Reflecting on these mistakes may be painful, but it's important for students to understand what went wrong so they can avoid them in the future.

An alternative taxonomy to Briceño's outlines the following three categories:

1. **Content mistakes:** These occur when we don't know some critical piece of information.

2. **Process mistakes:** These occur when we don't know how to approach a question—that is, when we lack the necessary skill (as opposed to lacking content knowledge).

3. **Careless mistakes:** These occur when we misread a prompt, try to do too much in our heads, are disorganized, and so on. These are similar to sloppy mistakes.

Using Mistake Journals in the Classroom

Keeping a Mistake Journal is a great way for students to track, analyze, and reflect on their mistakes. They can use their journals to keep a record of the questions or tasks where they made a mistake, categorize the types of mistakes they made, and note ideas for how to avoid the mistakes in the future. Start by creating a template that students can use for their journals. I recommend making a table in Google Docs or printing out pages of a spreadsheet. You can customize the template to suit your needs, but I would suggest using some variation of the headings shown in Figure 7.1.

Next, teach students how to complete their journals. The first thing they need to understand is the system they should use to classify mistakes. It's best if the whole class uses the same categories. Feel free to use the two classification taxonomies mentioned earlier in the chapter or

Figure 7.1

Sample Mistake Journal Headings

Date	Assignment	Question or Problem and Mistake	Category of Mistake	How the Mistake Happened

come up with your own. Once you've determined the taxonomy students will use, have them practice categorizing a variety of examples. Start by asking the class to discuss errors they commonly see. Then encourage students to look at their own work and classify some of their own mistakes. Conference with them individually and provide feedback to help ensure that they categorize their mistakes appropriately.

The next step is to ask students to accurately summarize the question that led to the mistake, then discuss with them how to identify what they need to learn to avoid the mistake in the future. This last task may be tricky at first. If students don't know what they don't know, it will be hard for them to articulate what they need to learn. Reassure them that they can always ask you to help identify gaps in their understanding. It is helpful to write a set of examples of journal responses or collect "exemplary" journal responses from students. Present these exemplars and discuss them as a group. Then ask students to complete a page of their Mistake Journal. As they do, check in with them individually and provide feedback. (Figure 7.2 shows an example of a completed Mistake Journal entry.)

Once students understand the process, make it a routine and regularly prompt your learners to update their journals. After students have been recording their mistakes in their journals for a while, facilitate a more holistic reflection. This can be done on a blank page in their journals. Provide some prompts that guide them to identify patterns in their mistakes, such as the following:

- What types of mistakes do you make most frequently?
- Is there a particular topic or unit that seems to especially give you trouble?

Figure 7.2

Sample Mistake Journal Entry

Date	Assignment	Question or Problem and Mistake	Category of Mistake	How the Mistake Happened
10/9/25	Add/subtract polynomials quiz	Question: $(5p^2 + 3p) + (2p^2 + p)$ Answer: $7p^2 + 3p$	A-ha moment	When I combined $3p$ and p, I thought it should just be $3p$ but p is actually like $1p$ so it should be $4p$.
10/9/25	Add/subtract polynomials quiz	Question: $(x^3 + 2x + 1) - (4x^3 + x^2 - 1)$ Answer: $-4x^3 + x^2 + 2x$	A-ha moment	Same mistake as above! I didn't realize that x^3 has a coefficient of 1 in front.
10/9/25	Add/subtract polynomials quiz	Question: $(x^3 + 2x + 1) - (4x^3 + x^2 - 1)$ Answer: $-4x^3 + x^2 + 2x$	Sloppy	I forgot to distribute the minus sign to all three terms in the second polynomial.
10/16/25	Add/subtract polynomials Unit test	Question: $(5y^3 + 2y^2) - (y^3 + y^2)$ Answer: $4y^3 + 3y^2$	Sloppy	I forgot to distribute the minus sign to both terms in the second polynomial.

- Are you following your own advice about how to make fewer mistakes?
- Is the frequency of your mistake-making increasing or decreasing? Why might that be?
- What have you learned from your mistakes?
- What have you learned through the process of tracking and reflecting on your mistakes?

An example reflection is shown in Figure 7.3.

Figure 7.3

Sample Mistake Reflection

On our first quiz, I was confused about how a term like x really has a coefficient of 1 in front so $x + 3x$ isn't $3x$, it's $4x$! This was an a-ha moment for me because I made the same mistake more than once, and after going over it with my classmates, I realized why I was confused. When I took the unit test, I didn't make this mistake again! However, I still made a sloppy mistake by forgetting to distribute the minus sign to all the terms. I need to be more careful about this. Maybe I should circle every minus sign so that I remember to pay better attention.

Occasionally, collect students' journals and review them. As you review, keep these questions in mind:

1. Are students diligently recording their mistakes?
2. Have they missed any mistakes that they should be paying more attention to?
3. Are they correctly categorizing their mistakes?
4. Do their reflections demonstrate that they have learned from the mistake(s) and thought about how to improve going forward?

Provide feedback to students about each of these categories, either in writing or in brief conferences with students.

Finally, create opportunities for students to share their mistakes. By discussing errors with their classmates, students will see that they aren't alone in their mistake-making. It is particularly helpful when students with a strong academic reputation share their mistakes, showing those who struggle that we *all* make them and reinforcing a healthy mistake culture.

These share-outs should be conducted in a low-stakes environment to avoid creating too much stress for students. For example, you might randomly pair students so they are only sharing with one student at a time rather than with the whole class, or invite students to choose three of their favorite mistakes to share. Since mistakes are kept in a journal, it shouldn't be too difficult for students to find meaningful examples, and by restricting the conversation to three mistakes, no one needs to know how many mistakes each student actually made. Allowing students to choose which mistakes to share also gives them some control over the conversation.

By encouraging students to reflect on their mistakes, you help them see that they're built into the learning process. Students will begin to see mistakes for what they are: common yet critical to growth in any area of their lives.

FAQs

Q: When should students write in their Mistake Journals?

A: You can ask students to log mistakes in their journals as often as you'd like. At the very least, I would recommend having them do so after major summative assessments such as unit tests, major essays, and high-stakes exams. However, you could have students reflect as often as every class period or on every piece of work that you return to them with feedback. It really depends on what time you have in your classroom.

Q: How can I integrate Mistake Journals into my routine?

A: One way to do this is to make it a station during station-rotation activities in your classroom. Another strategy is to dedicate time to reflection after returning a summative assessment. Many teachers spend a class period "going over the test" or giving students an opportunity to read through feedback on an important essay. Shift some of this time to have them reflect in their Mistake Journals.

Q: What if students struggle with writing in their journals?

A: If students struggle with journaling, allow them to try a different approach, such as by recording their own voices rather than writing or typing. If they are having trouble categorizing mistakes, you can set up individual meetings to give them further guidance.

Q: Should Mistake Journals be graded? How do I make sure students actually do this?

A: Many teachers try to get student compliance with class activities by attaching a grade to them. Mistake Journals should not be graded, but you should review them and provide feedback. You can hold students accountable through conferences or by having them share. Your feedback on their journals can also help them see whether they are being thorough and honest in their reflections.

Conclusion

Mistake Journals serve as powerful tools for helping students develop a reflective mindset and see mistakes as essential steps in the learning journey rather than failures. By recording, categorizing, and analyzing their mistakes, students can identify patterns, gain insight into their thinking, and take ownership of their growth. This practice not only deepens their understanding of the material but also nurtures a positive and resilient approach to learning. As students engage in honest self-reflection, they learn to appreciate their mistakes, transforming them from obstacles into opportunities for improvement.

When educators provide students with clear expectations, thoughtful reflection prompts, and structured feedback, Mistake Journals can become an integral part of a growth-centered classroom culture where mistakes are embraced, analyzed, and learned from—ultimately strengthening students' confidence and competence as lifelong learners.

In the next chapter, we'll examine how students can build community around mistakes by having regular Mistake Meetings together.

Additional Resources

- The article "Reflective Journals and Learning Logs" from Northern Illinois University's Center for Innovative Teaching and Learning outlines ways to help students start journals similar to the ones discussed in this chapter. You can find it here: www.niu.edu/citl /resources/guides/instructional-guide/reflective-journals-and -learning-logs.shtml

- Tara Schuster discusses and provides prompts for journaling in her article "Journal Prompts to Reframe Mistakes," available here: https://taraschuster.substack.com/p/journal-prompts-to-reframe -mistakes

8

Student Mistake Meetings

Once in high school, as I was presenting the solution to a linear algebra problem in front of the class, I misspoke and pronounced the word *seven* as "say-ven." My classmates cracked up. I was absolutely mortified and could barely continue. Even though the error had nothing to do with the content I was presenting, it kept me from volunteering to present in front of the class for the rest of the year. This happened more than 20 years ago, and I can *still* remember the brick I felt in my stomach as my classmates laughed at me.

Even though this is an example of a relatively minor moment of embarrassment, I share it to emphasize the significant impact that classmates' reactions to errors can have on students' willingness to take chances in school. Because a big reason we are so fearful of messing up in front of our peers is that we don't see how common mistakes are, perhaps we need more opportunities to put our mistakes out in the open, share them with one another, and develop a sense of belonging around our imperfections.

One way to do this is by having students hold meetings together to discuss their mistakes. If we are careful about how we facilitate such meetings, the power they can have on mistake culture is immeasurable.

How Mistake Meetings Help Students

Mistake Meetings break students out of their silos. When a student errs in isolation, they might feel like they're the only one who doesn't get it. The meetings allow students to see that their classmates make mistakes, too. Students should have the opportunity to choose which mistakes they feel comfortable sharing with their peers. Over time, they will likely be willing to share more and more of the mistakes they make as they see that they aren't being teased or laughed at. It can also be extremely validating for a student to see that a classmate has made the same mistake as they have.

I distinctly recall a Mistake Meeting in one of my classes when one student admitted he had overlooked the same step in a math problem that many others had struggled with, causing a wave of relief to come over the group. Almost instantly, another student exclaimed, "Yes! I did the exact same thing!" These students' reactions were filled with surprise and a hint of pride—they were glad to see they weren't alone in their missteps. They started comparing how they had each approached the problem and discussed where they'd gone astray. What began as a review of individual errors turned into a group brainstorm about strategies they could use to avoid this kind of mistake in the future. A few students who were normally quiet jumped in, saying things like "I actually thought I was the only one who messed this up." There was a sense of camaraderie in the room—a collective assurance that mistakes aren't personal failures but simply part of the learning process.

Mistake Meetings also provide students with an opportunity to learn from one another's mistakes. When students are exposed to mistakes that aren't their own, they see a much wider variety of errors—ones they may not have made themselves but plausibly could have made.

We've already talked about how we remember a concept better and learn it at a deeper level if we've made a mistake pertaining to it in the past. When students hear about the mistakes of their peers, the effect isn't quite as strong, but it still exists. When they need to recall the content in the future, they think, "Oh, yeah, Kyle said that he messed this up. I should be careful so I don't make the same mistake."

Implementing Mistake Meetings

Typically, Mistake Meetings are held at regular intervals throughout the year. Each 15-minute meeting follows a timed procedure with guided prompts to help students stay on track as they reflect on ways they learned from a mistake. First, they share the mistake with the group members, who silently review it. Then they explain the mistake and describe what they learned from it.

Start by dividing students into groups of three or four. I suggest keeping these groups consistent for at least a quarter so group members can bond and become comfortable with one another. Consider giving each student an index card and asking them to write down the classmates with whom they are most comfortable. When you divide up the students, keep those relationships in mind so the groups are already predisposed to be amicable. Students will not engage in the activity properly if they don't feel safe around the other group members.

After some time has passed, ask students for feedback on their groups and make any adjustments you feel are necessary based on what they report. Once the groups are established, students should follow the protocol shown in Figure 8.1. For the first meeting, however, they should avoid discussing schoolwork and instead talk about mistakes they've made outside school. Offer some examples of your own, such as using "Reply All" on an email when you meant to reply to only one person, texting someone you didn't intend to, or leaving a coffee cup on top of your car. This first meeting will help students understand the protocol while giving them a chance to get to know one another, laugh, and bond.

Figure 8.1

Mistake Meeting Protocol

Step 1: Introduction (2 minutes)

Designate one student to be the facilitator for the day. This role will rotate each meeting. The facilitator should welcome everyone to the meeting and explain the purpose: to share and learn from mistakes. They should emphasize the importance of learning from mistakes and how doing so contributes to personal growth.

Step 2: Sharing Mistakes (5 minutes)

One of the students shares a mistake they've made—either by showing the actual mistake or briefly describing it. This role should rotate each meeting.

Step 3: Silent Analysis (2 minutes)

After the student has shared their mistake, the group silently reviews and reflects on it.

Step 4: Explanation and Reflection (5 minutes)

The student whose mistake was analyzed explains what happened, why it was a mistake, and what they learned from it. Encourage them to reflect on what they would do differently in the future.

Step 5: Group Discussion (1 minute)

Group members share brief comments or questions. Encourage constructive feedback and supportive comments aimed at learning rather than blaming.

Step 6: Conclusion (1 minute)

The facilitator summarizes the key takeaways from the meeting.

Reinforce the idea that mistakes are opportunities for growth and improvement. Thank everyone for their participation and willingness to learn from one another.

Do what you can to ensure that the atmosphere remains supportive and nonjudgmental throughout the meeting. You should be circulating around the room the whole time, listening and looking out for any signs of distress. Time management is crucial. Make sure students stick to the time limit for each step and respect everyone's time. You don't want students to stew on a mistake for too long. Each student should have equal time so it doesn't feel like one student's mistake was "bigger" than anyone else's. You may want to consider using a timer.

FAQs

Q: What if the atmosphere turns negative?

A: Do what you can to minimize the chance of this happening by working hard to establish a warm and supportive classroom environment beforehand. Remember to keep the first meeting focused on getting students comfortable with one another.

You should also be circulating around the room throughout, listening for any negative turns and stepping in when necessary. A meeting might go astray simply because students don't know how to talk about mistakes. Model how to discuss mistakes constructively and without judgment. For example, if a student is responding negatively to another student's mistake, say, "I heard the feedback you just gave your groupmate. Let's work together to come up with a more constructive way for delivering it." Share these tips for ensuring that feedback is nonjudgmental:

- Phrase comments as questions instead of statements.
- If you do make statements, use the first person rather than second person to keep the pressure off the student sharing the mistake.
- Avoid generalizations.
- Focus on learning from the mistake.
- Offer support.

Q: What if students don't want to participate?

A: Students who don't want to participate in the activity might still feel a stigma around mistake-mistaking. Continue to do work outside the activity to improve the mistake culture in your classroom. Support individual students by brainstorming ideas with them before meetings so that if they come up with a mistake, they don't feel too vulnerable sharing.

Q: What if the mistakes students share are superficial?

A: At first, it's fine for students to share low-stakes mistakes. This will help them build comfort with the activity and with talking about mistakes. However, if students are still avoiding mistakes that they can actually learn from after several meetings, you may want to remind them of the purpose of the activity. Point out specific mistakes to individual students that you think they could learn from, and encourage them to share them at the next meeting.

Conclusion

Mistake Meetings offer a valuable opportunity to transform the way students perceive and respond to their own errors. By cultivating a space where students openly share, analyze, and reflect on mistakes, these meetings foster a resilient and growth-oriented classroom culture. Peers begin to see one another not as competitors but rather as allies in the pursuit of knowledge, making it easier for them to take risks and embrace errors as natural steps toward mastery.

In the next chapter, we'll examine test corrections—a popular strategy for encouraging a growth mindset and helping students learn from their mistakes.

Additional Resources

- Mindset Kit put together an entire minicourse about mistake culture that addresses how to implement and facilitate Mistake Meetings. You can find it here: www.mindsetkit.org/topics/celebrate-mistakes/importance-of-mistakes

- Jeff Miller's TED Talk "Why We Need to Talk about Mistakes" is a great resource about why it's important to discuss mistakes with others: www.cornerstoneondemand.com/resources/article/ted-talk-tuesday-why-we-need-talk-about-mistakes

9

Test Corrections and Revisions

I remember walking out of a test in high school and eagerly gathering with my friends in the lunchroom to compare answers. During those conversations, even before a friend pointed out a mistake I'd made, I'd smack my forehead in realization of some error that I only just noticed. Other times, I'd get a test back and sort through everything I had gotten wrong. I spent mornings, lunches, and afternoons in office hours with my teachers trying to understand my mistakes. (By contrast, some of my friends never revisited their old tests, assuming the extra effort wasn't worth it if it wouldn't result in an increased grade.)

Anytime these circumstances arose, the mistake I had made, the question that I got wrong, and my path to understanding became embedded in my memory. At the same time, I probably wouldn't have been able to tell you about a single question that I got right, how I learned the correct answer, or why it was correct. Today, I'd be more likely to make mistakes on the questions I had answered correctly than those I'd gotten wrong.

Test corrections and revisions give students the opportunity to revisit their mistakes and incentivize students to acknowledge where they went wrong, which in turn rewires their neural pathways so they lead to the correct answer.

It's important to note that test corrections and revisions play just a small role in the greater world of reassessment. Before students have a second opportunity to demonstrate learning by reviewing their errors, they need to understand the correct answers. In this chapter, we'll discuss revision practices that are particularly effective for improving learning and instilling a healthy mistake-making culture in your classroom.

The Benefits of Reexamining Mistakes

Students' learning need not end the moment they complete a summative assessment. As we guide our students to meet their learning objectives, we should offer them multiple opportunities to demonstrate their mastery of content. An important part of that process is allowing students to correct their mistakes on both formative and summative assessments.

Misunderstandings of content are both common and critical to learning. In fact, they are built into the four-stage learning cycle of concrete experience, reflective observation, abstract hypothesis, and active testing (Zull, 2023). For example, an apple falling from a tree provides a concrete experience. As we watch the apple and notice that it is no longer in the tree and has in fact taken a trajectory directly from its initial position to the ground, we are engaging in reflective observation. We may form the abstract hypothesis that all things that are dropped fall directly to the ground. We drop our hat to actively test this hypothesis. When we make a mistake that challenges our current understanding, we tend to form a new hypothesis and test it, which leads us to learn something new.

To learn from misunderstandings, students first need to know why they are incorrect. To ensure this happens, have students point to examples in their work that demonstrate a misunderstanding of the content. Then ask them to reflectively examine where they went wrong, note where the disconnect in their understanding is, and come up with a new line of thinking. The last stage of the learning cycle, active testing, occurs when students demonstrate that their new line of thinking leads to the correct answer.

Implementing the Strategy

Put simply, when students reexamine their mistakes, they should identify the

1. Type of mistake.
2. Line of thinking that led to it.
3. Thing they did to better understand the material.
4. Correct line of thinking for avoiding the mistake.

Let's go through each of these steps one by one.

Step 1: Students Identify the Type of Mistake

This is a good opportunity for students to use the mistake taxonomies discussed in Chapter 7. When students recognize the type of mistake they've made, they better understand how to avoid it next time. For example, a sloppy mistake could indicate a need to organize their work more cleanly on the page, an a-ha moment mistake could suggest they overlooked some important detail while learning the content, and a reach mistake could mean they are still misunderstanding the material and need to learn more to attain mastery.

Here's how two students in two different content areas might recount Step 1:

- **Math:** "I misinterpreted how to handle the order of operations in a complicated expression. I thought I could just go left to right without paying attention to the parentheses and exponents first, which led to an answer that didn't make sense. This was a reach mistake because I didn't really get the order of operations at all yet."
- **Social studies:** "I incorrectly stated that the Treaty of Versailles was signed before World War I and that it was the reason the war started. I didn't realize that the treaty was actually signed after the war ended, to formally bring peace. This was an a-ha moment

mistake because the timeline for the war finally clicked after I put it all together."

Step 2: Students Identify the Line of Thinking That Led to the Mistake

Ask students to explain why they thought their original answer was correct: "What was going through your head when you answered this way, and why did you believe you were right?" Reflecting on the flawed thinking that led to the mistake helps students better understand the content. Research shows that to correct a misconception, we need to know why our original thinking was wrong (Lucariello, 2025). Only when we are convinced that we genuinely made a mistake can we begin to repair our thinking.

This helps you as the teacher, too. When students explain their thinking, you gain a deeper understanding of where their misconceptions came from and can adapt instruction accordingly. For example, let's say the misunderstanding is due to the way a concept was taught in an earlier grade. In that case, you could work with the teacher in your building who teaches that grade to brainstorm a more effective approach to introducing the concept. Alternatively, if the misconception stems from your own teaching, you can revisit the concept with the whole class and make a note to address it more clearly from the outset next year.

Here's how the two students from Step 1 might recount Step 2:

- **Math:** "I was rushing and assumed that I could solve the problem just by doing each step as I saw it, going straight from left to right. I thought that addition, subtraction, multiplication, and division were all equal in priority, so I didn't realize that some operations needed to be done first. I wasn't really thinking about the order of operations in the proper way."

- **Social studies:** "I was confused because I remembered that the Treaty of Versailles was a big cause of tension between countries, and I thought it must have been one of the reasons the war started. I also assumed that because it's often discussed when learning about the causes of World War II, it must have been a major factor from the start."

Step 3: Students Identify What They Did to Better Understand the Material

Asking students how they were able to get the concept right builds accountability into the revision process and ensures that students put in the necessary effort. Some students will see a low score and immediately ask to revise, thinking that they will somehow magically do better this time around even though they haven't done anything to increase their understanding. Remind them that they need to put the time in if they want to truly master the concept.

Students should have access to resources such as textbooks and classmates to help them revise their understanding before retaking an assessment. If you don't give them access to learning materials, you send the message that they should just "try again" rather than take the time to truly understand the material.

To promote classmates helping one another, consider having your students plan to take every test twice: once on their own, then again with a partner (but without access to their independent work). This strategy forces collaboration and conversation about the content and any mistakes students might have made the first time around. One teacher who implements this strategy includes the results of both tests when calculating students' grades (Parker, 2024). It may not be necessary to include a grade for both tests, but you should certainly provide feedback on all the work, focusing on the new learning demonstrated from the first attempt to the second. Test corrections allow students to redeem their grades so they don't feel as though they're being punished for making mistakes.

Here's how the students from the previous two steps might recount Step 3:

- **Math:** "My teacher had me go over each part of PEMDAS: parentheses, exponents, multiplication and division from left to right, and then addition and subtraction from left to right. We worked through a few examples together where I could see the difference between the right way and my original approach. Then I practiced breaking down similar problems step by step and writing out each part to make sure I understood which operations had priority."

- **Social studies:** "My teacher had me go back through the timeline of major events in the early 20th century. I read about the causes of World War I and the aftermath separately instead of mixing up events from both wars. I paid close attention to the details of when the Treaty of Versailles was actually signed and why it led to future conflicts instead of starting the first war."

Step 4: Students Identify the Correct Line of Thinking for Avoiding the Mistake

This step comes last to emphasize the learning process rather than addressing the correct answer alone. This is also the most important step because it allows you to evaluate whether the student has actually gained a better understanding of the content.

Here's how our math and social studies students might recount this final step:

- **Math:** "The correct way to approach the problem was to focus on each part of PEMDAS in order. First, I needed to simplify everything inside parentheses, then handle exponents, and only after that go through multiplication, division, addition, and subtraction. By doing it this way, I got the correct answer because each operation happened in the right order, which helped me avoid adding and subtracting things too soon."

- **Social studies:** "The Treaty of Versailles was signed in 1919, after World War I, and it was meant to prevent future conflicts by setting strict terms for Germany. Instead, it actually increased tensions and contributed to the causes of World War II, not World War I. The correct understanding is that World War I started due to various alliances, militarism, and the assassination of Archduke Franz Ferdinand—not because of any formal treaty like Versailles."

Two-Step Process for Test Corrections

The two-step process for test corrections is a simple and effective way to implement this strategy.

Step 1: Students Prepare Corrections

In the first step, students prepare their test corrections on paper. I ask students to use a different-colored pen to analyze their original work. (If the work is digital, they can use a different-colored font.) They circle mistakes, write notes about what they were thinking when they came up with their answer, and classify their mistakes. Then they write their revised response either alongside the original or on a separate paper if they need more space to do so neatly. They also add a comment about why their new thinking is correct and how they know.

During this first stage, students can use any resources necessary to develop a better understanding of the content. I encourage them to consult one another, look back in their notes, ask me for help, and do any additional research they need to. These are all part of the process of learning.

Step 2: Student–Teacher Conference

During the second and final step, each student schedules a conference with the teacher. These conferences can occur during class, before school, at lunch, after school, in study hall, or whenever is most convenient.

The conference begins with the student explaining the mistake, their previous thinking, what they did to develop a better understanding, and how they arrived at the correct answer the second time around. As the student explains, listen carefully and ask probing questions. The work that they wrote down in the first stage is not the only reflection of what they really know; their words and demeanor during the conference can provide a much better sense of their handle on the material. A student who speaks quickly, stumbles, or sounds like they are reciting something they memorized may not have a deep understanding. One who can speak casually, calmly, and elaborate on their reasoning usually does have a good understanding. Next, I generate a new question for them to respond to that addresses the same concept (or even better, ask them to generate one themselves). They then answer the new question to give me further evidence of their mastery.

This protocol works wonders in my classroom. As students work on their written corrections, I see them engaged with all kinds of resources.

Often, students who didn't watch the videos I'd shared with them the first time around realize that they actually need to watch them and take notes. It's a brilliant opportunity for students not only to think about the content but also to reflect on what they need to do to truly master the content.

It's extremely difficult for a student to convincingly feign understanding when talking about content, so these conferences give me a good sense of how well they grasp the material. If they just memorize a few sentences and repeat them back to me, I know that their understanding remains shallow, and I can ask probing questions to discover what they still need to learn.

FAQs

Q: What if I don't have time for this?

A: Katie Harrison, curriculum coordinator for a school district in Delaware, works with teachers on their reassessment practices and says that finding the time is the most frequent challenge teachers face. In the case of test corrections, the solution is to empower students to provide one another with feedback and trust that, with the right guidance, they can do a good job.

You can also automate the process of providing feedback to clarify content. Harrison works with teachers who use a number-coding system for feedback that they give frequently. Instead of writing the feedback out, they use a number code and give students a cheat sheet explaining what each code means. Some subject areas might use the same codes to indicate the same comments. For example, in both English and social studies, a 1 might indicate a grammar or spelling error, whereas a 2 indicates an error in how a source was cited. Some codes might be subject-specific; for example, a math teacher might use a 1 to represent a mistake copying the problem down incorrectly.

Teachers can generate their own coding systems or collaborate within their department or grade-level team. Don't get too in the weeds by attaching a code to every mistake. Audit the mistakes you see and the comments you make to see which ones come up over and over again during the course of a unit or year. These are the comments worth developing a code for. You will still need to make specific comments on each student's paper tailored to their mistakes and the current content, and automating the most frequent ones frees up time to focus on those.

Another strategy for automating feedback uses a simple highlighter. Teachers make copies of a list featuring their most frequently used feedback. When they hand students back an assignment, they can also hand them a copy of the list with any pertinent feedback highlighted on it.

Q: What if students don't try on the first assessment because they know I'll allow corrections?

A: This is the most common concern I have heard from teachers about test corrections. It's very difficult to know the exact reason a student failed to perform well on an assessment, but allowing them an opportunity to correct their work helps them better understand the content. Try to make the process rigorous and compelling enough to deter lazy behavior. If students see the test correction as requiring just as much effort as studying the first time around, if not more, then they won't see it as an easy way out. They'll be more likely to put their best foot forward the first time so they won't be required to do so much additional work. Finally, if you also use the test corrections strategy for formative assessments, students will be more likely to do well on the summative assessment to begin with.

Q: How should I grade test corrections?

A: Grading test corrections is tricky, and every teacher will have to use their own expertise and experience to come up with a system that works best for them. Some teachers may decide to grade only the corrected test. Others will allow up to 50 percent of the points lost on the first test to be earned back through the retest. Still others will use both scores. It's up to you. Study your students and their motivation, consider your school's policies, and think about your values as a teacher to come up with a grading rule that keeps your students motivated and learning and that you're comfortable with.

As a rule, you should always reassess students to gauge mastery after they've had the opportunity to complete their corrections, especially if they use resources such as notes, peers, or a textbook to correct their work. A reassessment separate and apart from the test corrections ensures that students have integrated new learning to show their understanding. The reassessment could be the same format as the original or take a different format, such as a conference.

Katie Harrison says she has seen test corrections implemented most successfully when teachers remove "points" from the conversation and focus instead on verbal descriptors, perhaps aided by a single-point rubric with three columns: the middle column is the standard or learning target, the left column is for aspects of the former that the student has not yet mastered, and the right column is for the teacher to elaborate on how the student may have exceeded the objective. Such a rubric allows teachers to customize feedback so it targets exactly what the student needs to work on. Harrison further suggests targeting reassessments to only address standards or learning targets students haven't met.

Q: Don't I need to teach students to perform in a high-stakes environment where they won't be given an opportunity to redo what they've done?

A: Yes, students will encounter high-stakes environments where they will truly only have one chance. However, these situations are rare. Think about your own work environment: I'm sure you're able to seek feedback on and adjust many of your most important assignments. Besides, the reassessment following test corrections can offer higher stakes.

Q: How is this activity equitable? Why should a student who got it right the first time get the same grade as a student who needed multiple opportunities to get it? Why should a student who doesn't understand need to do more work than a student who does?

A: The focus should be on learning, not behavior. Katie Harrison suggests tasking all students in class with additional learning after they receive feedback on an assessment. For some students, this means getting a better handle on the original material. For others, it could mean engaging in an enrichment opportunity.

Students should also have a say in how to enhance their understanding of content. Harrison suggests providing them with a choice board like the one shown in Figure 9.1 and having them pick activities from either the learning options or the enrichment options.

Fostering an environment in which test corrections and revisions are integral to learning transforms mistakes into essential learning milestones. Test corrections encourage students to confront and reflect

Figure 9.1

Sample Choice Board

Learning Target	Learning Option 1: Video Review	Learning Option 2: Flashcards & Definitions	Enrichment Activity 1: Real-World Application	Enrichment Activity 2: Research Extension
Identify cell structures and their functions.	Watch a video explaining each cell part and its function; take notes on each part as you go along.	Use flashcards to memorize each cell structure and its function; quiz yourself or a friend.	Research how specific cell parts are affected by diseases (e.g., mitochondria in mitochondrial disease) and present your findings.	Choose a unique cell type (e.g., neuron, muscle cell) and research how its structure differs from typical animal cells.
Understand the difference between plant and animal cells.	Watch an animation showing side-by-side comparisons of plant and animal cells.	Make a T-chart comparing the features of plant versus animal cells using your textbook or notes.	Investigate how certain organelles (like chloroplasts) enable plants to produce their own food, and share your findings with the class.	Research unusual cells (like those in fungi or bacteria) and how they compare to plant and animal cells.
Explain how cellular respiration and photosynthesis work.	Watch a video tutorial that walks through each step of cellular respiration and photosynthesis.	Use flashcards to learn the key terms and chemical equations for both processes.	Explore how athletes rely on cellular respiration for endurance, and explain the role of mitochondria in energy.	Research the impact of photosynthesis on global oxygen levels and share how plants contribute to ecosystems.
Understand how cells divide (mitosis vs. meiosis).	Review a step-by-step video on mitosis and meiosis; make a diagram summarizing each step.	Use flashcards for key terms like *prophase, metaphase, anaphase,* etc., and explain each in your own words.	Research cell division disorders (e.g., cancer) and discuss how abnormal mitosis leads to health issues.	Investigate regenerative biology—how organisms like starfish and salamanders use mitosis to regrow lost parts.
Describe the role of the cell membrane in transport	Watch a video on cell membrane structure and transport methods (diffusion, osmosis, etc.).	Draw and label a cell membrane with its parts, showing where transport processes occur.	Research how cell membranes are targeted by certain medications (e.g., antibiotics) to treat infections.	Investigate recent research on cell membrane technology (like drug delivery systems) and present what you've learned.

on mistakes rather than see them as a final judgment on their abilities. By breaking the correction process into steps, we can help students form lasting understanding and self-awareness in their learning journey. When teachers support their reflection, we shift the classroom focus from simply achieving a grade to mastering content. This not only builds a more resilient and growth-oriented mindset in students but also encourages a culture where errors are seen as valuable steps in learning. Ultimately, incorporating test corrections and thoughtful reassessment can make education more equitable, fostering genuine understanding and skill development for all students.

Conclusion

Revisiting mistakes is an essential part of the learning process—one that helps students deepen their understanding and develop resilience. By guiding students through structured test corrections and meaningful reflection, we empower them to take ownership of their learning and grow from their errors. The strategies discussed in this chapter encourage students to analyze their mistakes, rethink their approach, and solidify their understanding through active engagement. When students see mistakes as valuable learning opportunities rather than failures, they become more confident, persistent, and ultimately more successful learners. In the next chapter, we'll discuss showing our appreciation for mistakes by literally putting them on display.

Additional Resources

- Scroll through this Reddit thread to find several teachers sharing their experiences with test corrections: www.reddit.com/r/Teachers /comments/dk9mn4/students_making_test_corrections
- Margaret McDade's Edutopia article "Using Test Corrections as a Learning Tool" suggests having students complete test corrections as a station activity and then retake the assessment: www.edutopia .org/article/test-corrections-high-school-math

10

Mistake Murals

As one of my favorite educators, Starr Sackstein, once shared with me, "What we dedicate time and space to in our classroom shows our students what we value." Her statement resonated with me and caused me to think deeply about what messages I inadvertently send my students via the walls and bulletin boards in my room.

I remember being in classrooms where bulletin boards were plastered with examples of student work that was absolutely perfect—no grammatical errors, aesthetically pleasing, not a single red mark from the teacher in sight. I desperately wanted to make sure that my work shined on those boards, too. Even after I became a teacher, I'd only put the "best" work on bulletin boards. If administrators walked in, I wanted it to look like my students were all knocking it out of the park all the time.

Walls that only display immaculate student work show that we value immaculate student work most. There are certainly some benefits to such displays; they provide students with models of exemplary work and can motivate them to do their best so their work can be displayed, too. On the other hand, these displays undervalue the messy process of learning. They discredit mistakes that happened along the way and fail to appreciate the value of those mistakes in getting to such beautiful final products. As I progressed in my teaching career, I began to include all kinds of work at all stages of completion on my walls. My favorite artifacts became those that showed scribbles, cross-outs, and all-caps a-ha moments.

This chapter discusses best practices for placing errors on display so students see that mistakes are valuable and worthy of our attention.

The Benefits of Mistake Murals

If you want to show your students that you value mistakes, dedicating space to a Mistake Mural in your classroom is a powerful way to send that message. Each student can contribute mistakes to the mural throughout the unit. Documenting each mistake requires them to reflect on the logic behind it, its value to learning, and the process of discovering the correct path. Reflections should be posted in a visually appealing way for all to see.

Creating a Mistake Mural is in line with the philosophy we have outlined for creating a positive mistake culture in the classroom. First, it shows that the teacher's response to mistakes is to value, honor, and celebrate them. Mistakes are uplifted and displayed rather than punished. Each student participates and therefore acknowledges that they are on a level playing field with their peers when it comes to making errors.

Students can also use the mural to study and learn from their classmates' mistakes. The mural can even serve as a teaching aid. When students make a mistake like one on the mural, you can direct them to "go look at the Mistake Mural" for ideas about what went wrong and how to fix it. In addition, students can use the wall as a reference when checking their own work before submitting it.

You can ask students to reflect on a mistake during the unit or as an end-of-unit exercise. When providing them with feedback on errors, you can say something like "This would be a really great example for the Mistake Mural."

Implementing a Mistake Mural

Follow these steps to use a Mistake Mural in your classroom.

Step 1: Students Select a Mistake to Add to the Mural

Have each student write a mistake on a small piece of paper or note card along with the following information:

- An illustrative example of the mistake being made. This could either be an exact copy of a mistake they made or a similar one that they create themselves.
- A description explaining the mistake in detail.
- A reflection on the line of thought that led to the mistake.
- A clear explanation of why the mistake is wrong.
- The correct answer.

You can also encourage students to incorporate visuals to help describe the mistake and its correction, such as flowcharts, illustrations, or annotated examples.

Step 2: Add Mistakes to the Mural

Next, add all the mistakes you receive to the mural. Arrange them in a visually appealing way and make sure the mural is visible and accessible to students. You can use a bulletin board, dedicated wall space, or another spot students can easily locate.

Step 3: Facilitate a Class Discussion

Once the mural is in place, facilitate a class discussion about it. Encourage students to share their findings, discuss the significance of each mistake, and reflect on the learning opportunities they presented. Emphasize the value of mistakes as learning opportunities. Discuss the concept of a growth mindset and how mistakes are essential for personal and academic development.

Mistake Trees

Consider having your mural take the form of a tree. Work with mistakes on it forms the roots of the tree; then, at the end of the unit, the leaves of the tree are populated with mistake-free work that was only possible thanks to lessons learned from analyzing the earlier errors. Here's how this might look in two different content areas.

History Example

- Roots
    1. A first attempt at a historical timeline in which students misplaced key dates or misunderstood cause-and-effect relationships.
    2. A cause-and-effect paragraph where students mixed up primary and secondary causes of an event.
    3. Prepared notes that demonstrate inadequate supporting evidence or weak reasoning.
- Leaves
    1. A corrected and revised version of the historical timeline with labels highlighting cause-and-effect relationships.
    2. An essay on a major historical event that accurately outlines causes and their effects.

Science Example

- Roots
    1. Initial attempts to calculate velocity and acceleration where students have misapplied formulas or units.
    2. A draft lab report on Newton's laws where students incorrectly identified action-reaction pairs or omitted units in their measurements.
    3. A problem set on forces showing math errors and incorrect free-body diagrams.

- Leaves
    1. A revised lab report with accurate data analysis and correct application of Newton's laws.
    2. A final problem set annotated to explain students' problem-solving processes and corrected free-body diagrams.

In each content area, the roots should represent authentic struggles and common mistakes that students make when learning the content. The leaves show the culmination of their learning—final assignments that would not have been as strong without the "roots" that helped them grow into mastery. This visual approach can make students' learning journey tangible, reinforcing that mistakes are essential to growth.

FAQs

Q: Can I grade students' contributions to the Mistake Mural?

A: Evaluate student work based on the clarity of their one-page descriptions, the accuracy of their analysis, the effectiveness of graphics used, and their ability to convey the importance of learning from mistakes. It's best for the grade to reflect only their understanding of the content, so although you may provide feedback on all these things, the grade should only reflect how well students understand the learning target as a result of the activity.

Q: Should student work be anonymous? Do parents ever get upset about their child's mistakes being on display?

A: Students may be hesitant to admit to their mistakes at first. If you find that they continue to be uncomfortable with sharing mistakes, you can keep their contributions anonymous. Over time, as your students redefine their relationships with mistake-making, they will hopefully be more willing to own their mistakes and prouder to share what they have learned from them. To get there, continue to use a variety of strategies to improve the mistake culture in your room.

I've never had an issue with parents being upset that their children's mistakes are on display. On the contrary, parents are often impressed to see the progress their kids are making. If a parent does take issue, explain the purpose behind the activity; if students are kept anonymous, let them know that as well.

Q: What if a student hasn't made any mistakes on assignments?

A: If you run into this issue, have the student reflect on "mistake traps" or near-mistakes—places where they might have messed up or where they caught themselves before making the mistake.

Q: How do I find the time to implement this strategy?

A: Rather than crafting the mural yourself during a prep period, you can save time by having students mount the note cards to the Mistake Mural themselves. They can collaborate on grouping similar mistakes together to create a sense of community around their errors.

Conclusion

Like the other strategies in this book, Mistake Murals help you shift your classroom culture to embrace mistakes as essential to growth and learning. By displaying errors alongside students' reflections and insights, we signal to students that errors are not only acceptable but also celebrated. A Mistake Mural serves as a testament to the learning journey, showing students that success is constructed on a foundation of honest reflection and lessons learned.

In the next chapter, we'll explore how drafting multiple-choice questions can help promote a healthy mistake-making culture.

Additional Resources

- Emelina Minero's Edutopia article "Learning Through Mistakes" discusses how visual displays can help students build the growth mindset to embrace mistakes. Read it here: www.edutopia.org/practice /embracing-failure-building-growth-mindset-through-arts
- Spark discussion about turning mistakes into beautiful art with this cute story and video: www.youtube.com/watch?v=l7GdbUZG09s

11

Student-Generated Multiple-Choice Questions

When I took my first 200-level courses as an undergrad, I quickly realized that I needed to learn how to study. Simply rereading notes and homework assignments was not as effective as it had been in high school. This required me to take a deeper look at the content through a new lens, teasing out what I thought was most important about it. The strategy that worked best for me was generating my own exam questions. I would comb through the material and attempt to predict what we would be asked. It was particularly satisfying when the questions I came up with actually appeared on the exams!

When we are asked to do something we've done before, there is very little pressure. We don't fear making a mistake because we already know the right answer. It is when we are asked to do something novel that we face uncertainty and anxiety. By trying to predict test questions, I was able to remove some of that uncertainty and go into my tests with more confidence.

The Benefits of Having Students Design and Reflect on Multiple-Choice Questions

Multiple-choice questions get a bad rap. It's true that answering them correctly isn't always indicative of deep understanding, but well-written multiple-choice questions can help show whether students truly grasp a concept or continue to harbor misconceptions about it.

Designing high-quality multiple-choice questions requires deep thought and a broad understanding of the topic at hand. Every good multiple-choice question has one single, clear, indisputably correct answer. The other options are called distractors. An effective distractor is an option that might seem correct at first glance but is revealed as wrong by further examination. Distractors are most effective when they reflect a common mistake or misconception related to the concept. Usually, there is one correct answer and three or four distractors.

Coming up with questions, distractors, and correct answers gives students insight into the process of assessment design and shows them that tests are literally designed to trick them into making a mistake. This understanding can help ease some of their anxiety when taking high-stakes multiple-choice assessments such as state tests, benchmark assessments, and college entry exams. Knowing how multiple-choice questions are constructed also helps students develop strategies for answering them correctly.

When students write their own questions, they reflect on the mistakes they made throughout the unit, transforming those errors into learning experiences. Students can compare their prior knowledge and misconceptions to what they've come to understand through practice and learning, reinforcing a growth mindset.

Developing Strong Distractors

Consider this multiple-choice question and set of answer choices:

Q: Why do we have seasons on Earth?
A. They are fun.
B. People get sick of winter.
C. So farmers get a break.
D. Earth is tilted on an axis. *(correct)*

Now consider this one:

Q: Why do we have seasons on Earth?
  A. Earth revolves around the sun.
  B. Earth is tilted on an axis. *(correct)*
  C. The distance between the sun and Earth changes.
  D. Earth rotates on an axis.

What do you notice when you compare the two sets of distractors? The first set is by a student who was asked to generate 10 multiple-choice questions about the seasons for an astronomy class. The second question is the student's revised version after being coached by the teacher to revise the answer options. When this student drafted the initial set, he knew what the right answer was and jotted down whatever came to mind to use as distractors. Most of these were silly and not plausibly correct.

The student's final draft reflects a deeper consideration of common misconceptions about seasons. His teacher coached him to think about his learning experience to generate the new distractors. She asked questions like "Why did you think seasons existed before we started the unit?" He responded that he knew it had to do with the sun, but that was about it. Then she asked, "When we learned about Earth orbiting the sun, how did your thinking change?"

He responded, "At first, we learned that as Earth orbits, sometimes it is closer to the sun and sometimes it's farther away. I thought that's why it was hotter or colder. But then we did that model where we realized it was the tilt, not the distance, that created seasons."

The teacher probed further, "What were some of the other things that confused you?" He thought about how he had mixed up Earth's revolution around the sun with its rotation on its own axis.

This discussion helped the student think much more deeply about what he'd learned over the course of the unit and ensure that all his misconceptions about the seasons were resolved.

Here's another example of a question with strong distractors:

Q: Which answer lists all the prime numbers between 0 and 10?
  A. 1, 2, 3, 5, 7
  B. 2, 3, 5, 7 *(correct)*
  C. 3, 5, 7
  D. 1, 3, 5, 7, 9

Each distractor in this case reveals something about students' misconceptions: answering A might mean they think 1 is a prime number, C might mean they think only odd numbers can be prime, and D might mean they are confusing prime numbers with odd numbers.

Implementing the Strategy

The first step in having students design multiple-choice questions and answers in class is to define the learning objectives or standards you want their questions to reflect. Explain what content you think they should have their questions address. This is a good opportunity to collaborate with students on reviewing the unit's most critical concepts. Then explain the purpose of the assignment to your class. Highlight the benefits, such as reinforcing their understanding, promoting reflection, and helping them recognize common mistakes and misconceptions around their learning.

Tell students how many question-answer sets you want each of them to write. Consider limiting them to five or so high-quality questions so they can put significant effort into each one. Show them examples and nonexamples of effective multiple-choice questions and distractors (see examples in Figure 11.1).

Constructing viable distractors means identifying the most likely mistakes students might make while answering each question. Consider scaffolding this process for students using a graphic organizer like the one shown in Figure 11.2. First, students write the questions they hope to ask in the first column. These should be based on the unit learning objectives. Next, they write the correct answer in the second column, consulting notes or the textbook to confirm it's really correct. Finally, in the third column, they write misconceptions they've had or that are common to the content.

After they have done some independent thinking, students can spend time talking with classmates and gather more misconceptions and mistakes that might help them devise distractors. Students will be less embarrassed to share their own mistakes and misconceptions if they see it as an opportunity to help their classmates. These discussions are also good opportunities to review and prepare for the unit's final summative

Figure 11.1

Examples and Nonexamples of Effective Multiple-Choice Question-Answer Sets

Criteria	Example	Nonexample
• Is the question easy to understand? • Does the question make sense? • Is the question asking for something specific?	Q: What is the main purpose of photosynthesis in plants? This question is straightforward and easy to understand, clearly asking for a specific concept.	Q: Why do plants do what they do with light and food? This question is vague and confusing, leaving the student uncertain about what is being asked.
• Is there only one correct answer? • Can you identify the correct answer easily based on what you've learned?	Q: Which gas is produced during photosynthesis? A. Oxygen *(correct)* B. Carbon dioxide C. Nitrogen D. Hydrogen Only one of the answer choices is clearly correct.	Q: What gases are involved in photosynthesis? A. Oxygen B. Carbon dioxide C. Both A and B *(correct)* D. Nitrogen This question creates ambiguity, making it hard to know if there's only one answer.
• Are the wrong answers plausible but clearly incorrect? • Do the wrong answers help you think about the question without confusing you?	Q: What organelle is responsible for photosynthesis? A. Mitochondrion B. Chloroplast *(correct)* C. Nucleus D. Ribosome Each option is plausible but clearly incorrect to a student who knows the content.	Q: What organelle is responsible for photosynthesis? A. Airplane B. Moon C. Chloroplast *(correct)* D. Shoe The distractors are nonsensical and implausible and do not help the student think about the correct answer.
• Is the question straightforward, without hidden meanings or confusing language?	Q: Which part of the plant absorbs sunlight for photosynthesis? This question is straightforward and clear.	Q: What is not a part of the photosynthesis process that does not involve light? The double negatives in this question create confusion and make it difficult to interpret.
• Is the question related to what you have learned in class? • Does the question cover important material from your lessons?	(For a unit on cell biology) Q: What is the function of the chloroplast in plant cells? This question is directly related to the topic of cell biology covered in class.	(For a unit that doesn't discuss historical figures) Q: Who discovered photosynthesis? If historical figures weren't discussed in the unit, this question is off topic.

(continued)

Figure 11.1

Examples and Nonexamples of Effective Multiple-Choice Question-Answer Sets (continued)

Criteria	Example	Nonexample
• Are all answer choices similar in length, level of detail, and structure, with no obvious pattern giving away the right answer?	Q: What is the primary energy source for photosynthesis? A. Water B. Sunlight *(correct)* C. Oxygen D. Soil nutrients All answer options are balanced in length and structure.	Q: What is the primary energy source for photosynthesis? A. Water B. Sunlight, which converts water and carbon dioxide into carbohydrates *(correct)* C. Oxygen D. Nutrients from soil The correct answer stands out due to its length and detail, giving it away.
• Are questions and answer choices free of spelling or grammar mistakes? • Are questions and answer choices well-written? Do they seem professional?	Q: What role does the mitochondrion play in animal cells? The question is free of grammar or spelling issues.	Q: What role do chloroplasts play in animal cells? This question seems unprofessional because it contains an error: chloroplasts do not exist in animal cells.
• Do the question and answer choices avoid dropping hints about the correct answer? • Are all answer choices presented equally without giving away the correct answer?	Q: What process takes place in the chloroplast? A. Photosynthesis *(correct)* B. Respiration C. Cell division D. Transcription This question is neutral and does not hint at the answer.	Q: What process, vital for plants to make food, takes place in the chloroplast? The phrase *vital for plants to make food* hints toward photosynthesis, making the answer too obvious.
• Is the question neither too easy nor too hard and at an appropriate level of challenge for students?	(For a high school biology class) Q: Which macromolecule is broken down in cellular respiration to produce energy? This question is challenging but appropriate for high school biology.	(For a high school biology class) Q: What is the powerhouse of the cell? This question is probably too easy for high school students.
• Is the language used in the question fair and unbiased? • Is the question free of any cultural, gender, or racial bias?	Q: What is the primary function of enzymes in biochemical reactions? This question is free of cultural or gender bias and accessible to all students.	Q: Why do Western scientists value the structure of cells so highly? The language in this question reflects an unsupported bias.

Figure 11.2

Multiple-Choice Question-Answer Set Graphic Organizer

Question	Correct Answer	Distractors
Why does Earth have seasons?	Earth's axis is tilted.	• Earth is sometimes farther from the sun. • Earth rotates on an axis. • Earth isn't a perfect sphere. • The sun is tilted. • The sun is sometimes brighter than other times.
Question	**Correct Answer**	**Distractors**
What river was crucial to the development of ancient Egyptian civilization?	The Nile	We learned about other civilizations that developed along rivers, like ancient Mesopotamia along the Tigris and Euphrates and Pakistan along the Indus. It's hard to keep track of which river is which.

assessment. When they have completed their graphic organizers, students can draw from the third column to create valid distractors. Make sure to provide feedback and coaching along the way.

Finally, have students separately submit well-developed solutions to each question they came up with. These solutions should describe why the correct answer is correct and why each distractor is not. As a fun extension of this exercise, consider compiling all students' questions into a practice test that you administer to the whole class. Each student will know the answer to the questions they themselves drafted but will be challenged by their classmates' questions.

FAQs

Q: Won't this activity reinforce wrong answers?

A: As we've discussed in previous chapters, generating mistakes on purpose is unlikely to reinforce wrong answers in the long run. As the correct answers are discussed and the incorrect ones are contrasted with them, students will learn more deeply by seeing both alongside one another.

Q: What if students can't come up with good questions?

A: If students struggle to generate good questions, you may need to provide additional scaffolding to support them. One way is to provide them with questions the first time. Spend time modeling how you came up with the questions based on the content, and have a class discussion about why the questions are interesting. Teach students about question taxonomy, depths of knowledge, open versus closed questions, and other aspects of question writing. Then have them generate multiple-choice options for each question.

The next time you do the activity, provide students with a bulleted list of topics and ask them to write a question about each one. You can provide them with a checklist (targeting criteria such as those in the first column of Figure 11.1) to evaluate the quality of their questions.

Q: What if students don't include a correct answer or continue to believe that one of the distractors is correct?

A: In either of these cases, it's clear that students still have a misconception about the content. Arrange to meet with them to analyze the disconnect in their understanding. Determine if you need to do some reteaching or provide them with additional learning opportunities.

Conclusion

Asking students to design multiple-choice question-answer sets challenges them to reflect deeply on their learning and misconceptions, transforming mistakes into tools for mastering new material. This activity not only builds content knowledge but also enhances metacognitive skills by asking students to consider why misconceptions happen and how they can be avoided. Writing plausible distractors encourages students to analyze common mistakes, thereby reinforcing correct answers while also improving test-taking strategies. When students understand how to construct effective multiple-choice questions and answer choices, they are better prepared to tackle exams with confidence, approaching each question with an informed, critical eye.

The next chapter describes a twist on this activity where every answer option is a distractor and students must answer the question "Which wrong is the most right?"

Additional Resources

- For a deep dive on multiple-choice questions, check out Glen Pearsall's 2018 ASCD book *Fast and Effective Assessment: How to Reduce Your Workload and Improve Student Learning*.
- This easy-to-digest page from the Center for Teaching & Learning at the University of Texas at Austin provides simple tips for writing high-quality multiple-choice questions: https://ctl.utexas.edu /multiple-choice-questions

12

Which Wrong Is the Most Right?

When I took AP Biology in high school, we regularly took multiple-choice exams to prepare for the AP test. I remember taking one exam that had a question about a population threatened by a natural disaster. The question was meant to address adaptations and genetic variation. When I read the response choices, I could not find one that seemed right. I read each response again and again. I tried to find the logic behind each possibility, racking my brain for the ways it might connect with what I believed to be the correct answer. I also tried to figure out what made all the choices wrong so I could convince my teacher that no correct answer was provided.

I spent at least 10 minutes on this question—far longer than I was supposed to. In the end, I discovered a flaw in my initial thinking. I was so set on believing my logic was correct that I hadn't thought carefully enough about the responses in front of me—and I had overlooked a vital misconception I held. Thinking about the question taught me something new. If I had believed that the correct answer were there to begin with,

I may not have thought so deeply. I wouldn't have tried to come up with convincing arguments for my teacher, and I wouldn't have discovered the truth in the process.

This chapter discusses ways to encourage deep thinking by providing students with multiple-choice questions that have no straightforward correct answer option. Students must think deeply about which choice is "most right" and justify their reasoning. By evaluating the logic and flaws behind each potential response, students are forced to examine subtle aspects of their learning by asking questions like

- What is the question really getting at?

- What is the essence of a correct response?

- In what ways does each option fall short of the right answer?

- In what ways does each option overlap most with the correct line of thinking?

After selecting the "most right" answer, students must justify their choice by explaining why it's closer to being right than the others. This exercise requires them to scrutinize each response individually rather than pass over the incorrect responses or randomly guess at the correct answer. If you have time, it is valuable to have the class discuss their responses and their justifications. These discussions could happen with the whole group or in smaller groups using a "think, pair, share" format. Hearing their classmates' reasoning can give students an even deeper understanding.

When every answer option is "wrong," students shift their focus away from choosing the right response toward critical thinking. They start to see that it's the reasoning and logic behind a response that matters most, and they become less worried about being perceived negatively by their peers because everyone chooses an incorrect answer. Furthermore, there is no punishment for selecting a wrong answer because that is the expectation for the activity. You can still grade the assignment, but the grade should be based on students' reasoning and justification for their choice rather than for what answer they chose.

Subject–Area Examples

The most challenging aspect of this exercise for teachers is to choose meaningful questions and answer choices. Ideally, questions will be similar to those that might appear on a genuine assignment or exam. Make sure answer choices reflect common mistakes or misconceptions that your students have had about the topic. The following are a few examples from different subject areas.

Social Studies

What is the capital city of Australia? Select the response that is the "most right."
A. Sydney
B. Melbourne
C. Perth
D. Brisbane

This question challenges students to recall an important fact about Australia. By presenting commonly mistaken cities as options, it encourages critical thinking and solidifies the "wrongness" of these answers, which will later help students discern the correct answer among incorrect alternatives. This question can also lead to an interesting discussion about what qualities a capital city should have: Should it have a large population? Should it be centrally located? Should it be a place where a historical event took place?

An example of a successful response to this question could be "Sydney is the best answer for the capital of Australia. Although it is not the capital, it is an important city in Australian history. It was the first British settlement in the country and is also the city with the largest population. Historically, it was almost named as the capital."

Another successful response could be "While none of these answers are correct, Melbourne is the 'closest' to the capital of Australia. I believe this because Melbourne was the capital of the Commonwealth of Australia until 1927. Therefore, in some ways, it was actually the capital."

Both of these responses could end with a discussion of the correct answer: "The true capital of Australia is Canberra. When the country was forming the Commonwealth of Australia, leaders tried to decide between Melbourne and Sydney for the capital. They compromised by building a new city: Canberra."

English Language Arts

Which of these passages is more right?
A. *The Great Gatsby* is a novel that's set in the Roaring Twenties, with parties and wealth. Then there's Gatsby who loves Daisy but she's with Tom, and the green light across the bay means something about dreams maybe. Everyone seems to be searching for something, whether it's love or money or status. It's like nobody really gets what they want, and the American Dream is questioned but not really defined, and there's this tragic beauty to it all.

B. *The Great Gatsby* explores the illusion of the American Dream by depicting the tragic life of Jay Gatsby who rises from poverty to immense wealth only to realize that money cannot buy happiness nor can it reclaim the past through Gatsby's obsession with Daisy Buchanan Fitzgerald illustrates how the pursuit of material success and social status often leads to moral decay and personal despair

The first passage does not make clear points and does not seem to have a central theme, but it has perfect punctuation. The writer seems to lack confidence and doesn't assert anything of substance. By contrast, the second passage is relatively clear and uses strong academic language. However, it lacks proper punctuation and is one long run-on sentence. Analyzing these examples can lead students to discuss the role of punctuation in writing as well as the importance of crafting focused paragraphs.

Math

Calculate: $9/5 \times 12/13$. Which answer is the best answer?
A. 0
B. 1/2
C. 3/2
D. 2

Though none of the answer choices are correct, this question encourages students to discuss strategies for rounding and estimating. Doing so helps them build number sense and test the reasonableness of answers they may come up with.

A successful response could be "9/5 is close to 2, and 12/13 is close to 1. Since 2 times 1 equals 2, the closest answer is 2."

Another successful response might be "9/5 is less than 2, and 12/13 is less than 1. When we multiply a number by a number less than 1, it gets smaller, so the closest answer would be 3/2 because that is less than 2."

Both of these responses demonstrate sound mathematical reasoning and estimation skills without actually solving the problem (which is not the point of this particular exercise).

Science

Which of the following is the closest to the definition of *acceleration*?
 A. Acceleration is when an object speeds up.
 B. Acceleration is speed.
 C. Acceleration is velocity.
 D. Acceleration is a force.

None of these options is correct, but each represents a misconception that students might have about acceleration. Many students confuse acceleration and speed. Students also may not understand that acceleration is a vector, meaning it has both magnitude and direction, and the direction can be both positive and negative.

One example of a successful response could be "The closest answer is that acceleration is when an object speeds up. This is close because acceleration is when an object changes velocity. It isn't completely correct because acceleration could also mean that the object is slowing down."

Implementing the Strategy

Once you have chosen your questions and answer choices, decide on the format for this activity. I recommend answering the questions as a whole class or small group. When sharing the questions, present them to students one at a time. I like to do this with a prepared slide deck and the

Poll Everywhere app. Have students think about the question before they select a response. If you use the app, you'll be able to display the distribution of choices. Review the answers as a class and then have a discussion. Ask, "Would someone who chose answer choice B please explain their reasoning?" Encourage healthy and respectful debate as students discuss the choices.

Class discussion allows all students to benefit from the logic and thinking processes that their classmates share, deepening their learning. All the multiple-choice options are of course incorrect, but if the question has a correct answer, wrap up the discussion for each question by talking about it. As research shows, learning from mistakes requires comparing and contrasting errors with the correct answers (Pillai et al., 2020).

FAQs

Q: How can I generate effective questions for this activity?

A: Remember that a good distractor is one that is plausible—or even better, one that students have previously believed was correct. You can collect wrong but plausible answers by asking students to answer fill-in-the-blank questions on homework assignments and using any wrong answers as answer options for the activity.

You can also try using an AI chatbot like ChatGPT to design answer options. Write a question and then ask the chatbot to "design four plausible but incorrect responses to the question." Of course, be sure to carefully vet anything that AI writes for you!

Here's how this worked when I tried it myself. The prompt I used was "Please generate four plausible but incorrect answers to the following question: 'What is the purpose of mitochondria?'"

Here were the responses:

- Mitochondria store genetic information and control cell division.
- Mitochondria produce lipids and proteins for cell membrane construction.
- Mitochondria are responsible for detoxifying harmful substances in the cell.
- Mitochondria regulate water balance within the cell.

Conclusion

By presenting students with wrong but plausible multiple-choice options and inviting them to choose the "most right" answer, we help them employ critical-thinking and problem-solving skills without fear of failure. The activity in this chapter encourages students to focus on their reasoning, weigh perspectives, and think deeply about their choices. By emphasizing the thought process over finding a single correct answer, students can appreciate that learning is often about exploring possibilities, testing ideas, and understanding nuances rather than simply getting things "right." It's a lesson in approaching life's inevitable gray areas with open-mindedness and thoughtful discernment.

In the next chapter, we discuss how to leverage student-teacher learning conferences to increase metacognition and ensure that students learn from mistakes.

Additional Resources

- Connie Malamed provides tips for writing plausible distractors here: https://theelearningcoach.com/elearning_design/tests/the-importance-of-writing-effective-distractors
- In this video, science teacher Emma Taylor explains how to uncover misconceptions in her particular subject area: www.youtube.com/watch?v=l22cf7XZT5s

13

Student–Teacher Learning Conferences

When I taught math in high school, students would regularly switch from AP Calculus to the non-AP version of the class partway through the first semester. Once there, these same students would often boast about being ahead of their new classmates. They'd say things like "I already learned that" or "You guys haven't done that yet?" The reality is they probably felt insecure about the fact that they'd dropped an AP course and wanted to prove to their peers that they were still "smart."

I remember noticing that these students rarely offered answers during board work or group work. They would make comments like "This is so easy" without actually contributing. It occurred to me that they were probably acting out of a heightened degree of mistake anxiety. Because these students felt vulnerable, their identity as "smart" was hanging in the balance, threatened by delivering a single wrong answer in front of their peers.

One student, Kevin, was a memorable case. Kevin worked hard to be seen as a model student. He participated on the student council and took as many AP courses as he could. When he dropped AP Calculus and entered my class, his peers were shocked. During the first few weeks, Kevin procrastinated and rarely made productive contributions. He told me that since he knew the material already, he didn't need to do the work; he just needed to review it before his next student assessment conference.

I began to worry that Kevin wasn't making progress, so I decided to proactively schedule his conference rather than wait for him to tell me when he was ready. During the conference, I prodded Kevin to explain the content to me so I could assess his understanding and determine if he was truly ready to move on. As he attempted to do so, I discovered many misconceptions and gaps in his knowledge that we needed to rectify. I gave him some targeted practice and told him to tell me when he was ready to conference again.

At the next conference, Kevin came in much better prepared. He was able to explain the content to me clearly and generate examples. At the end of the conference, I asked him, "What's a mistake you think you or one of your peers might make regarding this topic?" Because we had focused so much on misconceptions in the previous conference, he had a thoughtful response to this question.

As Kevin became more comfortable in class, he began offering more answers during group work and board work. Even when they were wrong, his contributions led to fruitful conversation. He also began helping his peers with their work and noticing the errors they made.

As time went on, I began asking all my students to reflect on mistakes they felt would be common for each topic during conferences. Each time, I could see them reflecting deeply on their experiences with the content, and they often offered exceptional answers. In this chapter, we'll discuss how to use student-teacher learning conferences to encourage students to focus on the importance of reflecting on mistakes and misconceptions.

The Benefits of Student Conferences

There is no better way to tease out students' understanding than simply by talking to them. In a conference setting, all students have an opportunity to thrive. Distracted students who struggle to focus on paper exams can articulate themselves and stay on task. Students who lack confidence can receive a little nod from you at each step to encourage them to keep at it.

Adaptability

Every conference looks different. All students address the same learning targets at the same depth of knowledge, but each conversation is unique. Students take the lead; though the teacher asks probing questions, students need to generate definitions, explanations, examples, and tasks that demonstrate their understanding of current academic standards. At the same time, successful assessment conferences are usually characterized by

- A consistent set of "need-to-knows" that the teacher determines in advance.
- Student-generated examples and justifications.
- Teacher support and feedback.
- Reflection and goal setting.

Focus on Student Thinking

Conferences allow you to assess students on so much more than just their ability to answer a question correctly. Discussions can focus on thought processes, mental schemas, and misconceptions. Probe student understanding with prompts such as "Explain this to me," "Tell me in your own words," and "What does this remind you of?" to make student learning visible.

Deeper Learning

Conferences allow you to challenge each student appropriately. By asking students to choose their own level of difficulty, you allow them to operate within their comfort zone so you can identify their depth of knowledge. If you feel they are ready, you can even push them to learn concepts beyond what they studied in class. When I probe deeper like this, I let students know that they are not being assessed on this part of the conference, which helps them feel safe taking risks, even if they are wrong. On the other hand, you can scaffold the assessment by using extra probing questions for students who need more support.

Sometimes a student knows something but doesn't know how to say it. In those cases, your role is to help draw the knowledge out of them. Try to build their confidence by saying something like "I think you get this, but I just need a little more evidence to be convinced. Let me ask you a few more questions." Soon, they start to realize that they understand more than they thought they did, which builds their confidence and helps them be less fearful of trusting their intuition in the future.

Feedback

We all know that effective feedback needs to be timely. In conferences, all the feedback is delivered instantly. When students make a mistake, you can correct them on the spot by giving a new example to help them notice their flawed thinking. If they are on the right track but lacking confidence, you can encourage them and validate their correct ideas.

Curiosity

In a conference, you can pick up on a twinge of interest and ignite it. For example, I remember one conference when a student asked if you could take derivatives for complex functions (functions on complex numbers), which led us down a winding rabbit hole.

Use the end of a conference as an opportunity for each student to make predictions about the upcoming unit. For example, in my math classes, I might show students a problem from the next unit and ask them how they think they would solve it to get them thinking about new information they'll need to understand down the line.

Accountability

Let's face it, it's hard to BS your way through an oral conference. The first year that I used conferences in my calculus class, one student tried to memorize the rigorous definition of a limit. When our conference began, she said, "Can I just write down the definition so I don't forget it?" This was a signal to me that she didn't truly understand the concept.

"Instead, can you give me an intuitive understanding of that definition?" I asked. When she couldn't, we both agreed that it would be better for her to prepare a little more before sitting down to conference with me.

Guidelines for Effective Conferences

To get the most of student assessment conferences, follow these guidelines.

Structure Learning Around Conferencing

Try to ensure that your conferences fit naturally into the flow of learning. As students practice and study in class, hold regular informal conferences where you ask them to explain what they are thinking. Provide formative assessment opportunities such as group work or board work to make students' thinking patterns visible. If possible, hold informal conferences daily and more formal ones every week or two.

Establish Conference Logistics

My assessment conferences take between 5 and 20 minutes, depending on how much content there is to assess. I prefer frequent conferences assessing smaller chunks of information over infrequent ones that cover a lot of content. Since students move at their own pace, it's rare that many students will all need a conference on the same day. One to three short conferences per class period with time to check in with students in between is a lot less logistically challenging than conferencing back-to-back-to-back for the whole period. It's also important that students know what they should be working on while you conference with their classmates.

Clarify Learning Goals

It's important to have an idea of what information you want to assess before each conference. An outline of learning goals helps ensure that conferences are equitable and match the depth of knowledge required by standards. To prepare for each conference, begin by breaking down the standards into bullet points and rewriting each one as a question (see Figure 13.1). Then determine which bullet points reflect need-to-knows and prioritize them. Plan for extensions and scaffolds.

Before finalizing the list, double-check to make sure that you've set the conference up to align with the questions you've planned. Finally, try to plan for the unknown. Consider all the ways a student might respond to each question. Ask yourself, "What are all the different ways 'mastering' this standard could look?"

Figure 13.1

Example of Turning Standards into Conference Questions

Original Standards	1. Represent data on two quantitative variables on a scatter plot and describe how the variables are related.
	
	  a. Fit a function to the data; use functions fitted to data to solve problems in the context of the data. Use given functions or choose a function suggested by the context. Emphasize linear, quadratic, and exponential models.
	
	  b. Informally assess the fit of a function by plotting and analyzing residuals.
	
	  c. Fit a linear function for a scatter plot that suggests a linear association.
	
	2. Interpret the slope (rate of change) and the intercept (constant term) of a linear model in context of the data.
	
	3. Compute (using technology) and interpret the correlation coefficient of a linear fit.

Bullet Points	• Students need to know vocabulary such as *independent* and *dependent variables, positive relationship, negative relationship, linear, scatter plot, correlation coefficient, slope,* and *residuals.* • Students must be able to fit a line to data. • Students must be able to estimate a correlation coefficient from a graph. • Students must be able to calculate a residual and explain how it is related to the correlation coefficient. • Students must be able to apply these concepts to data.

Essential Conference Questions	• When might you use a scatter plot? • Can you draw one? Make sure to label it with two appropriate variables. • Describe the scatter plot using the vocabulary you've been learning. • Estimate and interpret the correlation coefficient for your plot. • Draw a line of best fit and come up with the equation for it. • Interpret the slope and intercept of the line of best fit. • Calculate the residuals of a few of the data points. What do they mean? • Show me the data you've been using for your project. Which variables would be interesting to compare using a scatter plot? • Use Google Sheets to make a plot and add the line of best fit. • Interpret the plot. What does this actually mean in terms of the variables you chose?
Extension Questions	• Can you write the formula for calculating the correlation coefficient? How does it relate to residuals? • In what scenarios might a line <u>not</u> be the best way to make predictions? Let's look at some data. What types of non-linear models might best be used here? • Is the correlation coefficient applicable in these scenarios?

Start Broad and Conceptual

The learning targets assessed in each conference have an overarching theme or big idea. I like to begin each conference with general content questions that target the main points. These might include questions like

- What is the limit definition of a derivative?
- Can you give an intuitive explanation of _____?
- What did you learn about in this module?

Conceptual questions set the stage for the conference, and students' answers can give you a sense of whether they're ready. If they can't succinctly summarize the content, they probably need to prepare more and consolidate their ideas. Say something like "Are you sure you're ready to conference today? Do you want to spend a little more time trying to tie all these concepts together?"

If the student seems ready—and after establishing the big idea for the conference—ask higher-level questions such as these:

- How does what you learned in this module build on what you learned before?
- Why do you think you learned about limits before you learned about continuity?

Questions like this get students thinking broadly about the context of their current learning.

Dig Deeper

After asking broad and conceptual questions, move on to more specific ones. In math, this often involves doing some sort of calculation or demonstrating a skill. I typically ask students to come up with their own example of a way they might apply a skill they've been learning (e.g., "Come up with an example where you would need to use the quotient rule to find the derivative"). This allows me to see if they know both when and how to use the skill.

As students work on the problem, I ask probing questions like "How did you know to do that?" "Are you sure about that?" and "How would your process be different if . . . ?" to help clarify their thought processes.

Mistakes and misconceptions typically surface at this point in the conference. Rather than immediately point them out, wait for the student to finish working out the example. Sometimes, they notice it themselves. If they don't, ask questions that will help them identify where they went wrong.

Preview What's to Come

Conferences can serve as opportunities to preview what's to come and learn what students know about it. For example, if a student is sketching graphs of derivatives from a function graph, I might draw the graph of sine and ask them to use their curve-sketching skills to draw the derivative graph. Then I'll point out that they have just drawn the graph of cosine and therefore derived the fact that the derivative of sine is cosine—a fact they will be using in the next module.

End with Metacognition and Mistake Analysis

End the conference with metacognitive questions such as these:

- What was the hardest part of this module?
- Where did you notice yourself making the most mistakes?
- What types of mistakes could you see your peers making on this module?
- How did you check your work?

I love hearing what students say during this part of the conference. It's also awesome to hear how their responses evolve, increase in detail, and build on previous responses over time:

- "I thought I understood limits in the first module, but now I feel like I really understand why we need both the left and right limit."
- "I think the conference helped me sort out what piecewise functions really are and how they relate to the jump discontinuities we looked at in graphs."
- "I realized that my brain is always going a mile a minute and I can't talk fast enough. Coming up with an example helps me slow my brain down so I can explain."

FAQs

Q: When all your attention is on the student with whom you are conferencing, how do you make sure the other students stay on task?

A: My class is self-paced, and I ask students to set goals at the beginning of class so they know what they need to do. Even if you don't have a self-paced classroom, you can still design tasks that students can work on independently when you are in a conference. It also helps to face the room while conferencing. This allows you to occasionally glance up at the group and address any off-task students. Always plan time to check in with the class in between conferences. Consistently doing so lets students know that if they have a question, they can hold it until you're done with the conference. Empower a student to enforce norms or answer questions for you while you're busy with a conference.

Q: Conferences take a long time. Instead of everyone testing at once, you have to meet with each student individually. How do you make sure they're efficient?

A: Frontload some of the work. You can prepare questions or criteria in advance and make sure students prepare, too. A little preparation ensures that there is no "dead time" during a conference. Make sure students review any earlier assessments beforehand. You can also ask each student to fill out a Google Form before each conference to help them think about what they want to discuss. That way, you'll avoid hemming and hawing during the precious one-on-one time.

Q: How do you balance an authentic conversation with consistency in evaluation?

A: Conferences make it easy to fall into a trap of inconsistency. You might notice yourself giving a little too much support to one struggling student but holding back for another. You might push some students harder or get off topic to discuss something that has piqued both of your interests. This is why having a list of need-to-knows and sample questions is critical.

Preplan any scaffolds that you feel comfortable offering, but never offer more than you've planned during the conference. Only assess students on your preselected list of learning targets. If you are consistent about this core part of the conference, you can feel free to go off on tangents and push students further beyond it, so long as you do not assess items outside the list.

Q: What if other students cheat by listening in on their classmates?

A: It is difficult for students to copy their classmates when conferences are so personalized. However, if a student overhears something that leads them to prepare examples they want to use in advance, that's totally fine as long as they still learned the content!

Q: What do you do if a student is not prepared?

A: When a student needs more support or scaffolds than I am willing to give during an assessment, I use the one-on-one time to diagnose gaps and misconceptions and to suggest avenues for additional learning.

Q: Do conferences prepare students for the rigors of college or more formal exams?

A: Conferences do not necessarily replace traditional assessments. Students still take quizzes and write essays. They are supplementary exercises that allow students to explain how to do something or why something works the way it does. And by requiring students to reflect on their mistakes, conferences lead them to deepen their learning.

Q: Can you grade conferences?

A: My students and I decide on a grade together. I don't use percentage grades; instead, I ask them to rate themselves on a scale of 0 to 8 relative to each standard where 0 means they didn't explore the standard at all, 1–3 means they understand the basics of the standards and can grasp some parts with help, 4–6 means they need minimal support to demonstrate the standard, and 7–8 means they have mastered the standards and can demonstrate it without support. We each write the score we think the student deserves on a whiteboard. We discuss any disparities until we agree but don't say the scores out loud. Grades only reflect students' knowledge of the need-to-know items. Once we establish a grade, we have a conversation about whether and how they've reflected on mistakes and other aspects of their learning.

Conclusion

I've seen firsthand how powerful one-on-one student-teacher conferences can be in fostering students' confidence and deepening their understanding of content. The conferencing approach creates an individualized experience for students that shifts them from rote memorization toward meaningful engagement and growth. Students gain insight into their learning process, grapple with misconceptions, and reflect on the nuances of each topic, which can be challenging to achieve in a traditional classroom setting. Witnessing the progress students make through conferences has reinforced my belief that learning is about far more than getting the right answer; it's about understanding, adapting, and continually striving to improve.

Additional Resources

- Starr Sackstein is truly the hero of the student conferencing space. Her recent book *Student-Led Assessment: Promoting Agency and Achievement Through Portfolios and Conferences* explains how to integrate this incredible assessment technique into your daily practice.
- Middle school teacher Brian Hyosaka has a refreshing and personal take on student conferences that you can read about here: www.embarkeducation.org/blog/555-minutes-learner-centered-conferences

Conclusion

Fostering a positive culture around mistakes in my classroom has been one of the most transformative shifts I've made in my teaching practice. I vividly remember a moment with a student named Ella during a Mistake Meeting. Ella was a bright, thoughtful student who tended to crumble under the weight of her perfectionism. One day, as the class analyzed common errors on a challenging assignment, Ella hesitated, then bravely shared her mistake.

To her surprise, another student exclaimed, "Oh, my gosh, I did the same thing!" A ripple of relief spread across the room as more students chimed in with similar experiences. What began as a moment of vulnerability turned into an empowering discussion about growth, and I watched Ella's confidence bloom over the next few weeks. She began to approach challenges with curiosity instead of fear, embracing mistakes as part of her journey.

The 12 strategies outlined in this book offer a rich toolkit for addressing the fear of failure and helping students develop resilience, creativity, and a growth mindset. Which strategies resonated with you? Do you want to try adding in a few guessing games or a prediction activity? Can you start small by simply tweaking your feedback and the way you talk about mistakes? Would you rather implement a big change, such as introducing assessment conferences that allow you to talk about mistakes with students one-on-one? How will you begin to change the culture around mistakes in your classroom? I hope that you will return to this book to guide you along the way.

Remember, the journey toward fostering a positive mistake culture isn't linear, and you don't need to tackle every strategy at once. Start small, build momentum, and watch as your students begin to embrace their mistakes as stepping stones to success. Ella's story isn't an outlier—it's what happens when students feel safe, supported, and inspired to learn through their mistakes. That's a kind of magic worth cultivating in every classroom.

References

Briceño, E. (2015, January 16). Mistakes are not all created equal. Mindset Works. https://community.mindsetworks.com/entry/mistakes-are-not-all-created-equal

Cain, C. K., Blouin, A. M., & Barad, M. (2003). Temporally massed Cs presentations generate more fear extinction than spaced presentations. *Journal of Experimental Psychology: Animal Behavior Processes, 29*(4), 323–333.

Center for Innovative Teaching and Learning. (2012). Reflective journals and learning logs. Northern Illinois University. www.niu.edu/citl/resources/guides/instructional-guide/reflective-journals-and-learning-logs.shtml

Center for Teaching & Learning. (2022, May 8). Writing multiple choice questions. https://ctl.utexas.edu/multiple-choice-questions

Chiappetta, E. (2022, January 4). Using positive feedback in math classrooms. Edutopia. https://www.edutopia.org/article/using-positive-feedback-math-classrooms

Chiappetta, E. (2023, April 14). A collaborative approach to mistake analysis. Edutopia. https://edutopia.org/article/collaborative-approach-mistake-analysis

Cohen, Z. (2020, October 5). The taxonomy of mistake literacy: 7 levels of learning. Zak Cohen Education. https://www.zakcoheneducation.com/blog/the-taxonomy-of-mistake-literacy-7-levels-of-learning

Cyr, A.-A., & Anderson, N. D. (2018). Learning from your mistakes: Does it matter if you're out in left foot, I mean field? *Memory, 26*(9), 1281–1290.

Di Michele Lalor, A. (2022, June 24). Feedback that empowers students. Edutopia. https://www.edutopia.org/article/feedback-empowers-students

England, E. S. (Host). (2023, January 16). Normalizing failure with Zak Cohen (No. 90) [Audio podcast episode]. *Anchored in Education*. Apple Podcasts. https://podcasts .apple.com/us/podcast/normalizing-failure-with-zak-cohen/id1457633055?i =1000594663609

Harouni, S. L. (2022, August 25). Why am I afraid to fail? How our fear of failure can hinder growth. Take Root Therapy. https://www.losangelesmftherapist.com/post/why-am-i -afraid-to-fail-how-our-fear-of-failure-can-hinder-growth

Hyosaka, B. (2022, February 15). 555 minutes: Learner-centered conferences. Embark Education. https://www.embarkeducation.org/blog/555-minutes-learner-centered -conferences

Jacoby, L. L., & Wahlheim, C. N. (2013). On the importance of looking back: The role of recursive remindings in recency judgments and cued recall. *Memory & Cognition, 41*(5), 625–637.

Kawasaki, M. (2010). Learning to solve mathematics problems: the impact of incorrect solutions in fifth grade peers' presentations. *Japanese Journal of Developmental Psychology, 21*(1), 12–22.

KidsKonnect. (2021, August 16). 13 fun and educational guessing games for kids. https:// kidskonnect.com/articles/guessing-games-for-kids

The Learning Network. (2019, December 12). What students are saying about how to improve American education. *New York Times*. https://www.nytimes.com/2019/12/19/learning /what-students-are-saying-about-how-to-improve-american-education.html

Liljedahl, P. (2021). *Building thinking classrooms*. Corwin.

Litt, D. (2017, October 20). Why laughing at your mistakes is the perfect way to move past them [Video]. PBS. www.youtube.com/watch?v=5WJhEoHWKo4

Lucariello, J. (2025). How do I get my students over their alternative conceptions (misconceptions) for learning? American Psychological Association. https://www.apa .org/education-career/k12/misconceptions

Malamed, C. (2024, November 8). The importance of writing effective distractors. The eLearning Coach. https://theelearningcoach.com/elearning_design/tests/the-importance -of-writing-effective-distractors

Mangels, J. (2023, August 22). Don't erase that mistake. *ASCD Blog*. https://ascd.org/blogs /dont-erase-that-mistake

Marks, I., & Tobeña, A. (1990). Learning and unlearning fear: A clinical and evolutionary perspective. *Neuroscience & Biobehavioral Reviews, 14*(4), 365–384.

Marlett, D. (2024, October 23). Learning through mistakes: How deliberate errors can boost student engagement and retention. Learning-Focused. https://learningfocused.com /learning-through-mistakes-how-deliberate-errors-can-boost-student-engagement -and-retention

Marlett, D. (2024, January 25). Teaching students error analysis: A pathway to critical thinking. Learning-Focused. https://learningfocused.com/teaching-students-error -analysis-a-pathway-to-critical-thinking/#ELA

McDade, M. (2022, December 19). Using test corrections as a learning tool. Edutopia. www .edutopia.org/article/test-corrections-high-school-math

Merriam-Webster. (2004). *Merriam-Webster's collegiate dictionary* (11th ed.). Author.

Metcalfe, J. (2017). Learning from errors. *Annual Review of Psychology, 68*(1), 465–489.

Midwinter, A. (2014, March 14). My favorite no [Video]. https://www.youtube.com /watch?app=desktop&v=srJWx7P6uLE

Miller, J. (2025, April 9). Why we need to talk about mistakes [Video]. www .cornerstoneondemand.com/resources/article/ted-talk-tuesday-why-we-need-talk -about-mistakes

Mindset Kit. (n.d.). Celebrate mistakes. www.mindsetkit.org/topics/celebrate-mistakes /importance-of-mistakes

Minero, E. (2016, October 4). Learning through mistakes. Edutopia. www.edutopia.org /practice/embracing-failure-building-growth-mindset-through-arts

Palincsar, A. S., & Brown, A. L. (1984). Reciprocal teaching of comprehension-fostering and comprehension-monitoring activities. *Cognition and Instruction, 1*(2), 117–175.

Parker, J. (2024, March 11). Best way to do test corrections: Simple and engaging. Teach Every Day. https://teacheveryday.com/test-corrections

Pearsall, G. (2018). *Fast and effective assessment: How to reduce your workload and improve student learning.* ASCD.

Pillai, R. M., Loehr, A. M., Yeo, D. J., Hong, M. K., & Fazio, L. K. (2020). Are there costs to using incorrect worked examples in mathematics education? *Journal of Applied Research in Memory and Cognition, 9*(4), 519–531.

Roberts, S. L. (2016). Keep 'em guessing: Using student predictions to inform historical understanding and empathy. *Social Studies Research and Practice, 11*(3), 45–50.

Rushton, S. J. (2018). Teaching and learning mathematics through error analysis. *Fields Mathematics Education Journal, 3*(4).

Sackstein, S. (2015). *Teaching students to self-assess: How do I help students reflect and grow as learners?* ASCD.

Sackstein, S. (2024). *Student-led assessment: Promoting agency and achievement through portfolios and conferences.* ASCD.

Santagata, R. (2005). Practices and beliefs in mistake-handling activities: A video study of Italian and US mathematics lessons. *Teaching and Teacher Education, 21*(5), 491–508.

Schuster, T. (2024, June 9). Journal prompts to reframe mistakes. https://taraschuster .substack.com/p/journal-prompts-to-reframe-mistakes

Setiya, K. (2024, May 24). Go ahead and make fun of your friends. *The Atlantic.* https://www .theatlantic.com/books/archive/2024/05/david-shoemaker-wisecracks/678471

Shahbandeh, M. (2024, February 2). Per capita consumption of eggs in the United States from 2000 to 2024: Egg consumption by country 2024. https://worldpopulationreview .com/country-rankings/egg-consumption-by-country

Steuer, G., Rosentritt-Brunn, G., & Dresel, M. (2013). Dealing with errors in mathematics classrooms. Structure and relevance of perceived error climate. *Contemporary Educational Psychology, 38*(3), 196–210.

Taylor, E. (2020, December 11). Anticipating, uncovering, and reviewing misconceptions in the science classroom [Video]. www.youtube.com/watch?v=l22cf7XZT5s

Terada, Y. (2020, November 19). The mistake imperative: Why we must get over our fear of student error. Edutopia. https://www.edutopia.org/article/mistake-imperative-why-we -must-get-over-our-fear-student-error

Venet, A. S. (2021, November 11). How to give positive feedback on student writing. Edutopia. https://www.edutopia.org/article/how-give-positive-feedback-student-writing

Zull, J. E. (2023). *The art of changing the brain: Enriching teaching by exploring the biology of learning.* Routledge.

Index

The letter *f* following a page locator denotes a figure.

creativity, feedback to honor, 19–20
curiosity
    feedback to spark, 21
    igniting in student-teacher
        conferences, 108

eggs, average number eaten per year,
    29
embarrassment, avoiding, 50–51, 65
empowerment, feedback for, 22
engagement, guessing games for,
    29–30, 38–39

fear, alleviating with guessing games,
    31–33
feedback
    auditing your own, 25, 26f
    automating, 78–79
    celebrating growth and
        perseverance, 20–21
    coding systems, 78–79
    constructive, 21–22
    demonstrating value, 19
    detailed, benefits of finding time
        for, 27
    to empower, 22
    examples, 17–18
    honoring creativity, 19–20
    ineffective vs. effective examples,
        23–25
    a learning opportunity, 23
    Mistake Journals, 62, 63
    positive, 27
    promoting deeper thinking, 21
    providing the right amount of,
        22–23
    shaping understanding, 18–19
    sparking curiosity, 21
    in student-teacher learning
        conferences, 108
    timely, 22–23, 108

grading
    content-aligned prediction
        activities, 37–38
    guessing games, 31–32
    Mistake Journals, 63, 87
    student-teacher learning
        conferences, 115
    test corrections, 79–80
growth, feedback to celebrate, 20–21
to guess, defined, 29–30
guesses
    grading, 31–32
    judging, 31–32
guessing games
    criteria to alleviate fear, 31–33
    for engagement, 29–30, 38–39
    unfair prompts, revising, 33f
    variety in, strategies for, 38

journals, benefits of, 56. *See also*
    Mistake Journals

learning
    feedback for, 23
    from mistakes, 7–8, 49–50, 72–73
    reflection and, 57–59

meetings. *See* Mistake Meetings
mistake analysis
    in action, 41–44
    in asynchronous online settings, 47
    basic structure, 40
    benefits of, 44–46
    effective, 40–41
    ego in, 46
    large class sizes, 46–47
    My Favorite No activity, 50–54
    participation in, encouraging,
        46–47
Mistake Attitudes Survey, 13f
mistake culture, healthy
    building a, 10–12, 14–15, 46,
        117–118

About the Author

Emma Chiappetta has been an educator for the last 12 years. She has taught all levels of math from 6th grade to college as well as engineering and robotics. Emma has worked with teachers across all disciplines in her work as the director of faculty development at Wasatch Academy and as a mastery coach for Mastery Portfolio.

Emma sees herself as a learner and constantly tries new things with her students. She frequently asks for their feedback, learns from her own mistakes, and adapts lessons for each individual student. In her work with both students and teachers, Emma strives to personalize learning journeys in accordance with their individual strengths, curiosities, and goals.

Emma is a passionate writer and loves to share everything she has learned throughout her journey as an educator. She has written extensively for Edutopia and a variety of other blogs and recently published her first book, *Creating Curious Classrooms* (ConnectEDD).

Outside her work in schools, Emma can be found rock climbing with her husband Zeb, reading to her daughter Xyla, solving crossword puzzles, doing yoga, or baking sourdough bread.

Related ASCD Resources: Classroom Culture

At the time of publication, the following resources were available (ASCD stock numbers in parentheses).

Better Days: 180 Creative Practices and Daily Connections for Teachers and Students by Lisa J. Lucas (#125013)

Fast and Effective Assessment: How to Reduce Your Workload and Improve Student Learning by Glen Pearsall (#118002)

Results Now 2.0: The Untapped Opportunities for Swift, Dramatic Gains in Achievement by Mike Schmoker (#123048)

Small but Mighty: How Everyday Habits Add Up to More Manageable and Confident Teaching by Miriam Plotinsky (#125003)

Student Learning Communities: A Springboard for Academic and Social-Emotional Development by Douglas Fisher, Nancy Frey, and John Almarode (#121030)

Teach for Authentic Engagement by Lauren Porosoff (#123045)

Understanding Your Instructional Power: Curriculum and Language Decisions to Support Each Student by Tanji Reed Marshall (#122027)

For up-to-date information about ASCD resources, go to www.ascd.org. You can search the complete archives of *Educational Leadership* at www.ascd.org/el.

For more information, send an email to member@ascd.org; call 1-800-933-2723 or 703-578-9600; send a fax to 703-575-5400; or write to Information Services, ASCD, 2111 Wilson Boulevard, Suite 300, Arlington, Virginia 22201, USA.

An ASCD Study Guide for *Learning by Mistake: 12 Strategies to Turn Student Errors into Opportunities*

Emma Chiappetta

This ASCD Study Guide is meant to enhance your understanding of the concepts and practical ideas presented in *Learning by Mistake*, an ASCD book written by Emma Chiappetta. You are encouraged to use this study guide as you finish each chapter. The questions are designed to help you make connections between the text and your professional situations and experiences, plus apply what you learn. Although you may think about these questions and tasks on your own, you might consider pairing with a colleague or forming a study group with others who are reading *Learning by Mistake*. The study questions and tasks provided are not meant to cover all aspects of the book but, rather, to address specific ideas for implementation and discussion.

Chapter 1: Creating a Positive Mistake Culture

1. Begin some conversations with your students about their attitudes toward mistakes. Start with the question that I did: "What is it like to make a mistake at school?" Then reflect on the patterns you notice in their responses.

2. Reflect on your own attitudes about mistake-making. How do you feel when you make a mistake? What do you do next?

3. Consider the four levers that affect mistake culture in the classroom: consequences, teacher reactions, teacher strategies, and peer reactions. Audit your own classroom.

    a. What are the consequences of mistakes in your class?

    b. How do you typically react or respond when a student makes a mistake?

    c. What strategies do you already use to help students get over their fear of mistakes?

    d. How do other students in the class react when one of their peers makes a mistake?

4. Now that you have begun to research the current mistake culture in your classroom and explored your own personal attitudes about making mistakes, what do you hope to take away from this book?

Chapter 2: Addressing the Fear of Making Mistakes

1. What qualities do you notice about the prompts for the Wrong Answers Only activity?

2. Brainstorm some or your own prompts for the Wrong Answers Only activity. Do they satisfy the qualities you listed above?

3. What role do you think humor plays in mistake culture?

4. Take the mistakes attitude survey yourself. What do you notice? How do you expect students to respond?

5. Once you have taken the survey, edit it so it suits your context.

Chapter 3: The Effects of Teacher Feedback on Mistake-Making

1. What feedback has left you feeling shut down?

2. How can you use your own reflections to build empathy for how students will respond to what you say?

3. Look at the examples of feedback that does not promote a positive culture around mistakes—as well as the revisions. Practice revising them yourself.

4. Audit your feedback. Use Figure 3.1 (p. 26) to analyze the feedback you give your students. Use the third column to make revisions.

5. Expand the activity above by pairing with a colleague to improve feedback. Read this chapter and observe each other's classrooms. Discuss the feedback given and how students responded to it. Brainstorm how you can both provide feedback that helps to create a positive mistake culture.

Chapter 4: Guessing Games and Prediction Activities

1. Why are guessing games helpful to mistake culture?

2. How can prediction help students become more comfortable with being wrong?

3. How do you currently use guessing and predicting in your class(es)?

4. How can you expand or adapt what you are already doing so that it helps build comfort around mistake-making?

5. What types of guessing and predicting activities would make sense for your class? After reading this chapter, take time to brainstorm some ideas.

Chapter 5: Collaborative Mistake Analysis

1. What is the benefit of students generating mistakes *on purpose* rather than simply analyzing mistakes presented to them by the teacher?

2. Are your students aware of their mistakes?

3. How can you help students become more reflective about their mistakes so they are able to generate ideas for the activity?

4. How do your students typically behave during collaborative activities? Is there already a base level of trust, or do you need to build one before implementing this strategy?

5. Pick a topic for which you think this would be a good lesson to try. Anticipate the mistakes your students might generate as well as those you want to bring up during the discussion following the third round.

Chapter 6: Analyzing the Mistakes of Former Students

1. Think about mistakes you have made that have been made public versus those you keep to yourself. How do the feelings differ?

2. Use your own reflections to think about how students feel when they see their mistakes being shown to the whole class. How can you mitigate that?

3. My favorite "nos" are those where students are right on the cusp of understanding—where understanding the mistake is the last puzzle piece that needs to be set in place to paint a full picture. What are some of your favorite "nos"?

4. What student mistakes have you seen that are interesting and lead to deeper learning?

5. How can students benefit from mistake analysis both in their learning and in their attitudes?

6. Pick a unit or learning target that you know well. Which mistakes or misconceptions would you want to highlight with mistake analysis?

7. Can you use this activity to create a culture where students are proud to have their mistakes shared with the class?

Chapter 7: Mistake Journals

1. What routines do you already have in place for reflection?

2. How can you integrate mistake reflection into those routines?

3. Why should students reflect on mistakes?

4. What are some examples of the following, either from your own life or that you've observed your students make?

   a. A-ha Moment Mistakes

   b. Stretch Mistakes

   c. High-Stakes Mistakes

5. Why does having a taxonomy help students more effectively reflect on mistakes?

Chapter 8: Student Mistake Meetings

1. Have you ever talked about your mistakes with others? How did you feel during and after the conversation?

2. How can reflecting on your own experience talking about mistakes help you prepare for student emotions that may arise during mistake meetings?

3. Practice the mistake meeting protocol with your colleagues. Are there any aspects you would like to change or clarify before rolling it out with students?

4. How can you help students be reflective about their mistakes so they are prepared to share during the meeting?

Chapter 9: Test Corrections and Revisions

1. What policies do you currently have in place around test corrections and revisions?

2. Do your current policies support a positive mistake culture? Why or why not?

3. Why do we need to reexamine our mistakes?

4. Why is it useful to think about the flawed reasoning that led to a mistake?

5. How will you support students and provide opportunities for relearning as they revise their mistakes?

6. What is your plan or policy for grading revisions? Think about what is best for creating a healthy mistake culture, but balance that with the schoolwide policies in place.

Chapter 10: Mistake Murals

1. What do your classroom walls currently say about what you value?

2. Do you have space in your room for a mistake mural? If not, can you still send a positive message about mistakes using wall space?

3. Are there other ways you can demonstrate to students that mistakes are valued in your shared learning space?

Chapter 11: Student-Generated Multiple-Choice Questions

1. How does writing multiple-choice questions connect with mistake culture?

2. What are the qualities of good distractors?

3. How does the concept of a "distractor" connect with the idea of mistakes?

4. How can you support students in writing effective multiple-choice questions?

5. How can you ensure that students spend time thinking about the correct answer as well?

Chapter 12: Which Wrong Is the Most Right?

1. How and why does providing students with only wrong answer choices alleviate mistake anxiety?

2. How does providing students with only wrong answer choices affect learning more broadly?

3. Read the example questions given. What do you notice about them?

4. What are some common misconceptions you could highlight with this activity?

5. Try to create a few example questions and responses to try with your class.

Chapter 13: Student-Teacher Learning Conferences

1. How do one-on-one conferences support a healthy mistake culture?

2. Even if you can't fully implement conferences, make a plan for finding time to talk one-on-one with students about their mistakes.

3. If you do have time for a conference, prepare for one.

   a. Choose a standard to assess.

   b. Break it down into clear learning goals.

   c. Write opening questions that get at the main idea for the conference.

   d. Write questions that dig deeper.

   e. Plan some scaffolding questions for students who may be struggling, as well as some extension questions to spark curiosity and anticipation.

   f. Plan metacognitive questions that probe into reflection about mistakes.

Learning by Mistake: 12 Strategies to Turn Student Errors into Opportunities was written by Emma Chiappetta. This 125-page, 6″ × 9″ book (Stock #125011; ISBN-13: 978-1-4166-3382-2) is available from ASCD for $23.96 (ASCD member) or $29.95 (nonmember). Copyright © 2025 by ASCD. To order a copy, call 800-933-ASCD (2723) or visit ASCD at https://shop.ascd.org.

Transform Instruction to
Transform Students' Lives

Our Transformational Learning Principles (TLPs) are evidence-based practices that ensure students have access to high-impact, joyful learning experiences.

Endorsed by AASA and NASSP, the TLPs provide a shared language and a framework for reimagining teaching and learning, focusing on nurturing student growth, guiding intellectual curiosity, and empowering learners to take ownership of their education.

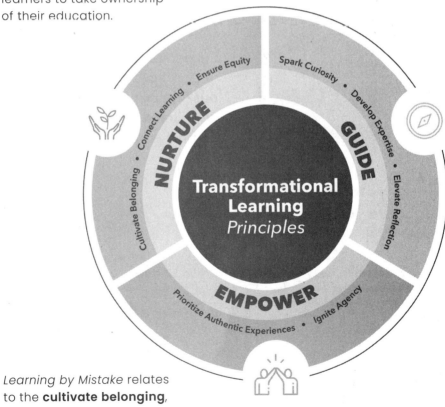

Ensure Equity • Connect Learning
NURTURE
Cultivate Belonging

Spark Curiosity • Develop Expertise
GUIDE
Elevate Reflection

Transformational Learning *Principles*

EMPOWER
Prioritize Authentic Experiences • Ignite Agency

Learning by Mistake relates to the **cultivate belonging**, **elevate reflection**, and **ignite agency** principles.

Learn more at **ascd.org/tlps**